Pelican Books
Know Your Own

D0448011

Dr H. J. Eysenck is Professor of Psychology in the University of London and Director of the Psychological Department at the Institute of Psychiatry (Maudsley and Bethlem Royal Hospitals). He was previously a psychologist at the war-time Mill Hill Emergency Hospital. He has lectured in many countries, and been Visiting Professor at the Universities of Pennsylvania and California. Known mainly through his experimental researches on the nature of personality he has written some three hundred articles in technical journals, as well as several books. These include *Dimensions of Personality*, *Know Your Own I.Q.*, *Check Your Own I.Q.*, *Description and Measurement of Personality*, *The Scientific Study of Personality*, *The Structure of Human Personality*, *The Psychology of Politics*, *The Dynamics of Anxiety and Hysteria*, *The Uses and Abuses of Psychology*, *Sense and Nonsense in Psychology*, *Fact and Fiction in Psychology*, *Sex and Personality* and *Psychoticism as a Dimension of Personality* (written with Sybil B. G. Eysenck). He is Editor-in-Chief of the journal *Behaviour Research and Therapy*.

Glenn Wilson has lectured widely in Britain and abroad, has spent some time at the London University Institute of Psychiatry researching into personality and abnormal psychology and held four visiting appointments as Associate Professor of Psychiatry at the University of Southern California Medical School, Los Angeles. He has published about eighty articles and several books, including *The Psychology of Conservatism*, *Improve Your I.Q.*, *Love's Mysteries: The Psychology of Sexual Attraction* (with Davis Nias).

Dr H. J. Eysenck and Glenn Wilson are co-authors of *The Experimental Study of Freudian Theories* and *A Textbook of Human Psychology*.

HANS EYSENCK AND GLENN WILSON

KNOW YOUR OWN PERSONALITY

PENGUIN BOOKS

Penguin Books Ltd, Harmondsworth, Middlesex, England
Penguin Books, 625 Madison Avenue, New York, New York 10022, U.S.A.
Penguin Books Australia Ltd, Ringwood, Victoria, Australia
Penguin Books Canada Ltd, 2801 John Street, Markham, Ontario, Canada L3R 1B4
Penguin Books (N.Z.) Ltd, 182–190 Wairau Road, Auckland 10, New Zealand

First published by Maurice Temple Smith 1975
Published in Pelican Books 1976
Reprinted 1978, 1979, 1981, 1982

Made and printed in Great Britain by
Hazell Watson & Viney Ltd, Aylesbury, Bucks
Set in Linotype Baskerville

CONTENTS

ACKNOWLEDGEMENTS

Cartoons 1, 2, 3, 5, 6, 9, 10, 11, 13, 14, 15, 17, 18, 19, 21, 23, 25, 26, 27, 29 and 30 are reproduced by permission of Punch Publications Ltd. Cartoons 4, 8, 12, 16, 20, 24, 28 and 32 are reproduced by permission of Bourne of Harlesden Ltd. Cartoons 7, 22 and 31 are reproduced by permission of Weekend Publications Ltd.

INTRODUCTION

The ancient Greek philosophers had a word for it: 'Know yourself.' This is good advice. Because of our limited knowledge, it is difficult to make rational choices in education (What should I study?), in choosing a job (What occupation or profession should I go into?), in love (What sort of woman/man would I be happy with in marriage?), or indeed whenever we have to make some important decision about our future. Professional psychologists see over and over again people who make the wrong choices, although it is quite obvious to the outsider that the choice is indeed very wrong; only too often this wrong choice is caused by erroneous self-perceptions, that is, a failure of the person concerned to 'know himself'. As Robert Burns expressed it so much more clearly:

> O wad some Pow'r the giftie gie us
> To see ourselves as others see us !
> It wad frae mony a blunder free us,
> And foolish notion.

It is the point of this book to help readers to see themselves as others see them, in a more objective light; whether this will free them from 'mony a blunder' and protect them from 'foolish notions', we cannot of course guarantee. This book takes its place beside *Know Your Own IQ* and *Check Your Own IQ*, both of which tried to do the same thing for the reader's intellectual abilities; but here we shall be concerned with personality rather than with intelligence. As in those other books, a short introduction will be given in which the concepts used are explained, the method of construction of the tests is outlined, and interpretation of the results is indicated. In fact, the tests are self-explanatory and the scoring will also be found quite easy; nevertheless, readers may find it useful to read through these introductory pages before going on to the actual tests.

Before we can describe or measure personality, we must have some sort of model to represent it, and some sorts of concepts to encapsulate the different aspects of the model. The ancient Greeks used a *type* theory; indeed, the four types of the sanguine, the phlegmatic, the choleric and the melancholic man have passed into popular speech. The observations on which these descriptions were based were very astute; even now we can recognize particular types falling into these groups. But they were wrong in postulating that everyone would constitute an example of one type or the other; most people in fact combine aspects of two or more types, and thus fall between the four classificatory baskets. The theory of the four types had a long history, lasting for some two thousand years; it was not finally abandoned until the beginning of this century.

Modern psychologists prefer *trait* theories to type theories. Traits are descriptions of habitual behaviour patterns, like sociability, or persistence, or impulsiveness. Such terms are very widely used in common speech. There are in fact some 4,500 trait names in use in English and although some of these are really synonyms, or sufficiently alike in meaning to refer to much the same sort of behaviour, a pretty large number of traits are left for the psychologist to use. Again, many of the remaining ones are quite specialized, or relatively unimportant; still the task of sorting out the remainder is quite a daunting one. Readers would have little cause to thank us if we simply printed a list of some 4,000 trait names in this book and left them to get on with it as best they could!

What psychologists have done, in principle, has been to group trait names according to the similarity of the names themselves or of the behaviour they refer to, and then to construct questionnaires to measure the central core of meaning underlying the groupings. A questionnaire is simply a list of questions relating to personal behaviour, preferences, reactions, attitudes and opinions; after each question is printed a 'Yes' and a 'No' (sometimes a '?' is also included for the 'don't knows') and the person filling in the questionnaire has to note down which answer is the right one for him. There is of course no generally right or wrong answer, as there would be for an intelligence test problem. If the question is 'Do you have many headaches?' clearly different people may give different answers without any implication that one answer is 'right' and the other 'wrong' (although of course it may be more pleasant for a person to be able to say 'No' rather than 'Yes'.)

Questionnaires come in all sorts and sizes, and it is important to differentiate between the journalistic playthings which are sometimes printed in popular newspapers and weeklies, and scientifically constructed and validated inventories having serious pretensions to measuring some meaningful aspect of personality. Anyone can string together a series of questions and call the resulting collection a questionnaire; what is it that differentiates the scientific inventory from the popular questionnaire? The simplest answer would be that the journalistic questionnaire is not based on a well-established theory, is made up of subjectively chosen questions without any effort to demonstrate their appropriateness or validity, and is not standardized on an appropriate population. It can be amusing, but should clearly not be taken seriously.

A properly constructed questionnaire is quite different. A great deal of work goes into the construction of the underlying theory, the selection and testing of the different questions, and the standardization on representative samples of the population; much effort may also be expended on trying to demonstrate that the questionnaire actually measures what it is intended to measure. All these points may benefit from a brief explanation to show just what is implied.

We may start with the construction of some sort of theoretical model of personality. We postulate a number of traits which we consider it would be interesting to measure, say sociability, impulsiveness, risk-taking, emotional expressiveness, reflectiveness, responsibility, physical activity; we then write a number of questions which we consider to be related to each of these traits. After a considerable amount of pre-testing, in which the reactions of many different people of varying standards of education and intelligence to the questions are recorded, a final list is made and administered to large groups of people. We now look at their answers, with the following consideration in mind. Suppose we are trying to measure sociability, and we take any two questions which we have included in the inventory. These might be: 'Do you like going to parties?' and 'Do you find it easy to enter into a conversation with people you don't know?' A 'Yes' answer would be keyed as scoring points towards high sociability. But that assumes that both questions measure the same variable (sociability) and that means that the majority of those who say 'Yes' to one question should say 'Yes' to the other; similarly, most of those who say 'No' to the one should also say 'No' to the other. This is an essential requirement; if the two questions are completely independent, then clearly they are not measuring the same entity!

It is easy to demonstrate statistically that for these two questions this requirement is met, and of course the questions are similar enough to make this almost a foregone conclusion. However, in other cases there may be more doubt; and conversely, we often find that items are correlated when on a priori grounds one might not have predicted it. The detailed statistical analysis of how the items relate to each other is an absolutely indispensable part of the construction of a proper questionnaire. Items that do not correlate with the remainder of the questionnaire must be eliminated, however inviting they may seem from the outside; only in this way can we obtain a homogeneous set of items all measuring the same trait. It is often necessary to try hundreds of items before one ends up with a set that shows sufficient differentiation from item to item (one does not want all the items to be too similar, obviously) and yet also shows sufficient homogeneity to enable one to state with some certainty that all items are clearly relevant to one particular trait. Common sense is a partial guide to good item selection, but common sense is wrong too frequently to be relied on very much; the statistical check is indispensable.

Let us assume we have constructed a number of questionnaires, dealing with a number of traits such as those enumerated above; we must next find out if these in turn are independent of each other. We might argue, using common sense, or experience, or empathy as our guide, that sociable people might be more impulsive than unsociable people, or that impulsive people might be more likely to take risks, or that physically active people might be less reflective and responsible than others. Clearly there is a possibility that different traits might not be entirely independent, and the discovery of correlations between traits is another task that psychologists have set themselves and have pursued with much application over the years. The outcome has been very clear-cut; there are many quite marked correlations between different traits, and these in turn therefore need to be incorporated into the theory. In order to do this, psychologists have used a hierarchical model.

This model is shown in Figure 1, in diagrammatic form. We have linked up the seven traits we have been measuring; they all correlate, in the sense that people who are sociable are also impulsive, active, risk-taking, expressive and lacking in reflectiveness and responsibility. This combination of traits gives rise to a more general, more inclusive trait, that of extraversion; in other words, extraversion is defined in terms of all the traits which can be empirically demonstrated to correlate together. It is possible to call extraversion a *type*, but this more modern use of the word does not carry any implication that everybody is either an extravert or an introvert. Rather, the term is used in the sense that there is a continuum from one extreme to the other, with the majority of people nearer the centre than the extremes. In fact, people are distributed along this continuum rather as they are on the continuum of height, or intelligence; few are very tall, or very bright, and few are very small, or very dull. Quite a few are tall, or bright; quite a few are small, or dull. Most are of medium height, or of average intelligence. From now on we shall use the term 'type' in this modern sense, not the old-fashioned sense of denoting exclusive groups.

Most people will know the terms extraversion and introversion through their association with the Swiss psychiatrist C.G. Jung, a former disciple of Freud who later on set up shop on his own account and was eliminated from the ranks of the disciples by Freud himself. Actually, the terms have a long history; they occur already in Dr Johnson's original English Dictionary, although with a rather different meaning. In the

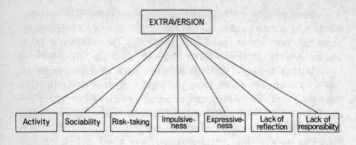

Figure 1

nineteenth century, however, they were already used in their present sense (or one very much like it) by novelists and others. Jung himself borrowed the terms to denote certain very complex personality characteristics which have little to do with observable behaviour; he also subdivided the psyche into four components, any of which could be extraverted or introverted. And, as if this was not complicated enough, he postulated that for each of these four functions there existed an unconscious form which was the opposite of the conscious one. In other words, if your feeling function, or your thinking function, was introverted consciously, then it would be extraverted unconsciously. The theory is so bewildering in its complexity that at the present day very few if any psychiatrists or psychologists use it, or take it seriously.

Extraversion-introversion is one modern type concept; are there others? There is considerable agreement among the many workers in this field that two other type concepts have been discovered and are well supported by the evidence. (There is less agreement on how these type concepts should be named; psychologists have always been rather prickly about using each other's nomenclature and consequently on first looking into the literature the reader may get the impression that everybody deals with different concepts. One soon gets used to the fact that they are talking about much the same traits and types. Our choice of terms in this book is consequently to some extent arbitrary; several other terms could have been used. This is of no consequence, of course; a rose by any other name. . . .)

The second type concept we shall be concerned with is called emotionality, or anxiety, or lack of adjustment, or instability, or neuroticism (or indeed any of a number of other terms). It too is based on the fact that various traits are empirically found to correlate together; Figure 2 shows that the type is made up of the traits of low self-esteem, lack of happiness, anxiety, obsessiveness, lack of autonomy, hypochondriasis, and guilt feelings. Correlations between these traits are of course not perfect, but there is an undoubted tendency for people who give high scores on one of these traits to give high scores on the others.

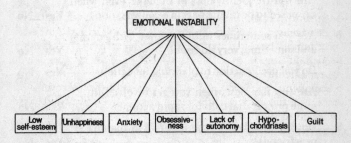

Figure 2

Before turning to our third typology, the reader may like to see the sort of questions which define these types, and the sort of relations that can be found between the questions in a typical sample of the population. Consider then the twelve questions in the accompanying questionnaire. (The number is of course much too small to give very meaningful results, but this brief questionnaire is given merely for the sake of illustration. Some of the actual questions used will be found again in questionnaires later on.) Before turning to the key, answer these questions for yourself.

Questionnaire

1   Do you sometimes feel happy, sometimes depressed, without any apparent reason?   Yes   No

2   Do you have frequent ups and downs in mood, either with or without apparent cause?   Yes   No

3   Are you inclined to be moody?   Yes   No

4   Does your mind often wander while you are trying to concentrate?   Yes   No

5   Are you frequently 'lost in thought' even when supposed to be taking part in a conversation? Yes   No

6   Are you sometimes bubbling over with energy and sometimes **very sluggish**?   Yes   No

7   Do you prefer **action** to planning for action?   Yes   No

8   Are you happiest when you get involved in some project that calls for rapid action?   Yes   No

9   Do you usually take the intiative in making new friends?   Yes   No

10 Are you inclined to be quick and sure in your actions?   Yes   No

11 Would you rate yourself as a lively individual?   Yes   No

12 Would you be very unhappy if you were prevented from making numerous social contacts?   Yes   No

Now for the scoring. A 'Yes' answer in any of the first six questions scores one point towards emotionality, while a 'No' answer does not score at all. Similarly, a 'Yes' answer to any of the last six items scores one point towards extraversion. You can therefore end up with two scores, either of which may run from 0 (very stable, very introverted) to 6 (very unstable emotionally, very extraverted). The majority of people will have scores of 2, 3 or 4; these indicate middling degrees of emotionality or extraversion.

How do we know that these questions fall into two independent groups and can be used for additive scoring? The answer lies again in the statistical device of calculating correlations; when this is done we find that the first six questions correlate highly together, and so do the other six questions. There is no correlation at all between the first set of six and the second set. This position is shown rather nicely in Figure 3 where the correlations between the twelve questions have been plotted diagrammatically. An angle of ninety degrees indicates no correlation at all, while an angle of zero degrees indicates perfect agreement. It will be seen that the two groups of six dots each are at right angles to each other, indicating that they do not correlate with each other. The six questions making up each of the two type questionnaires are very close together, indicating very high correlations among those in each group. Thus there is nothing subjective about our putting questions into different groups; this grouping is determined by the objective facts of the clustering of answers given by representative samples of the population.

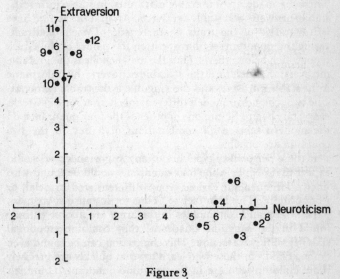

Figure 3

It would, of course, be ideal if questions could be found that range themselves so clearly into groups. Unfortunately, this is not so; there are many questions which are relevant to two (or even more) traits or typologies. This is not an insuperable statistical problem; we can count such a question twice (for each of the two traits it correlates with) or we can set it off against another question scored in the opposite direction, or we can just use it for the one trait and disregard its correlation with the other — doing the same in the opposite direction with another item also correlated with both traits. There are many problems of this kind which arise in questionnaire construction, but it would take us too far to discuss them here. The point is that psychologists are well aware of these problems and have worked out ways and means of dealing with them.

If we take our two types together, we obtain a model which actually shows some relationship to the old Greek model of the four temperaments. This is shown quite clearly in Figure 4, where the two dimensions or axes, extraversion-introversion and emotional stability-instability, define four quadrants. These are made up of unstable extraverts, unstable introverts, stable introverts and stable extraverts. Around the rim we have written some of the traits characteristic of each quadrant. Inside the quadrants we have written the names of the Greek types which belong there. Thus the melancholic is the unstable introvert; the choleric is the unstable extravert; the phlegmatic is the stable introvert; and the sanguine is the stable extravert. The two schemes or models differ mainly in that for the Greeks everybody had to fit into one or other of the four quadrants; on the modern scheme all combinations of scores on the two continua are possible.

If these personality types are of any importance, we would expect that people in the four quadrants would be found with unequal frequency in various groups differentiated on social, or work criteria. This is in fact so. Thus for instance sportsmen, parachutists and commandos in the army are almost entirely found in the sanguine quadrant; they combine emotional stability with extraversion. This connection can be found even among children; those who learn to swim quickly are precisely those children who are in the sanguine quadrant. Criminals

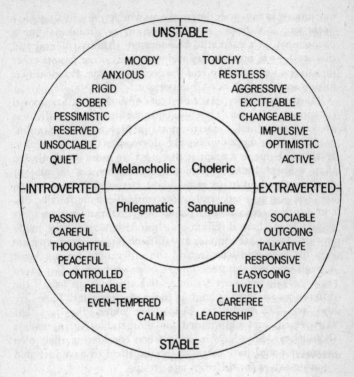

UNSTABLE

MOODY	TOUCHY
ANXIOUS	RESTLESS
RIGID	AGGRESSIVE
SOBER	EXCITEABLE
PESSIMISTIC	CHANGEABLE
RESERVED	IMPULSIVE
UNSOCIABLE	OPTIMISTIC
QUIET	ACTIVE

Melancholic · Choleric

INTROVERTED — EXTRAVERTED

Phlegmatic · Sanguine

PASSIVE	SOCIABLE
CAREFUL	OUTGOING
THOUGHTFUL	TALKATIVE
PEACEFUL	RESPONSIVE
CONTROLLED	EASYGOING
RELIABLE	LIVELY
EVEN-TEMPERED	CAREFREE
CALM	LEADERSHIP

STABLE

Figure 4

tend to be found in the choleric quadrant, neurotics in the melancholic quadrant. These two groups are apparently almost equally unstable emotionally, but for the most part the criminals are extraverted, the neurotics introverted. Scientists, mathematicians and successful businessmen are frequently found in the phlegmatic quadrant; clearly their phlegmatic behaviour does not extend to their work! None of these connections are absolute of course; they are tendencies, although fairly clear and powerful ones. Nevertheless, not all criminals are 'choleric', nor all cholerics criminal! It is important to see these things in perspective; personality is only one among many other determinants which result in a person's becoming a neurotic, or a sportsman, or a criminal, or a parachutist, or a successful businessman. Ability (mental and physical), luck, opportunity and very many other factors enter into the choices involved and the decisions made. Personality is important, but it is not all-important.

The third of our types is called toughmindedness, as opposed to tendermindedness. The traits entering into toughmindedness are aggressiveness, assertiveness, achievement-orientation, manipulation, sensation-seeking, dogmatism and masculinity. It will not come as a surprise that men are more toughminded than women! Indeed, there are sex differences on all our typologies and on many individual traits as well; thus women are less extraverted and more unstable emotionally. In comparing their scores with the norms, female and male readers should keep these differences in mind; it would have made scoring much more complex and difficult had we given separate keys for men and women and the differences are not large enough to make this necessary, though we have in fact given separate keys for our tests on sexual attitudes, in which the differences are large enough to make this essential. There are also age differences; as people get older, they get less extraverted, less toughminded, and more stable. Again, readers should bear these facts in mind when considering their own scores; it would have taken us too far afield to have included separate tables for different age groups.

Figure 5

Figure 5 shows the structure of toughmindedness, as composed of the seven different traits already enumerated. Toughmindedness, just like the other type concepts already discussed, is neither good nor bad in itself. Unlike intelligence, which is almost wholly 'a good thing', personality qualities are much more difficult to evaluate. Obviously there are many good points about the extravert; he is sociable, cheerful, always on the go; he likes people, and likes being with people. He is good company, tells jokes, often has charm, and generally puts life into social occasions. All this makes him a social asset. On the other hand, he is often unreliable, changes friends and sex partners frequently, is easily bored, finds it difficult to get on with uninteresting or time-consuming jobs. The introvert is the opposite of all this; from the work point of view, he would be much preferable unless the work involved other people, as would be the case for a salesman, for instance. Thus there is no way in which we could say that the extravert is superior or inferior in general to the introvert; they are just different. Each has his area of superiority and inferiority; what is important is that he or she should realize this and build on his or her *strengths*, and try to work round his or her weakness.

It might be thought that what was said above was not true of emotional instability; this might be thought to be wholly undesirable. To say this would be a gross exaggeration. Strong emotions are certainly likely to create difficulties for their possessor; however, they may also be of great help in achieving certain things. In one study of exceptionally creative visual artists, it was found that, as compared with the average sort of person, or even not so original and creative artists, every one of the successful group scored high on emotionality (and introversion). It almost seemed as if the great art these people produced was wrung out of a strongly emotional personality. Emotions can also serve to motivate a person; in this sense it may be very useful to have strong emotions in order to keep you going. After all, to be lacking in emotion is not ideal either; such people may lack many desirable experiences, and fail to make much of their lives. What is important is to know just where you stand; once you know whether you have strong, unstable emotions, are just an ordinary, average sort of person, or lack any emotional urge, you can plan your life in the light of this knowledge. 'There is nothing either good or bad, but thinking makes it so'—the saying is particularly apt when we look at different personality traits; almost all can be used to advantage, or abused to the harm of others and of the person concerned.

What does seem to come out from much of the research reported, however, is that extremes in personality can cause considerable difficulties. Very high or low scores on any personality trait or type suggest an imbalance in the person which is not necessarily fatal, but which needs considerable care in handling. This care is more likely to be forthcoming when the person concerned knows about his personality and the lack of balance; it is when this knowledge is missing that damage can be done. And of course the dangers presented by the possession of strong personality traits can also be used to advantage; they are rather like the gifts bestowed on baby princes and princesses in fairy stories by sorcerers and fairy queens. There is a certain ambiguity about these gifts, and great care should be taken about their use.

If we do not like our personality, can we not change it? Admittedly, most people seem to be quite fond of themselves, and think reasonably highly of their own personality. This is perhaps just as well; introverts often like and prefer introverts, and extraverts like and prefer extraverts as the ideal sort of person. How terrible if the position were reversed and everyone preferred the opposite personality type to himself! This would not be so bad if we could really do much about changing our personality in any fundamental sense; alas, this is not so. Personality is determined to a large extent by a person's genes; he is what the accidental arrangement of his parents' genes produced, and while environment can do something to redress the balance, its influence is severely limited. Personality is in the same boat as intelligence; for both, the genetic influence is overwhelmingly strong, and the role of environment in most cases is reduced to effecting slight changes and perhaps a kind of cover-up.

There is little point here in entering into a long discussion of the evidence for this statement, but readers are entitled to know in brief at least why we can say this sort of thing with some confidence. In the first place, then, it is quite generally found that identical twins (who have identical heredity are very much more alike in personality than are fraternal twins (who share only half their heredity). This is true even when the identical twins are brought up in separation, in different families; oddly enough, identical twins brought up in different families are, if anything, slightly more alike than are identical twins brought up in the same family, together. Furthermore, there is considerable concordance for neurosis and criminality in identical twins; in other words, when one twin is neurotic or criminal, so in all likelihood will be his identical twin. In the case of fraternal twins, however, concordance is very much less. This is just what would be expected on the hypothesis that heredity played a vital part in the production of individual differences in personality, criminality and neurosis.

Studies of adopted children have shown that as far as personality and intelligence are concerned, these children, even though taken from their biological parents just after birth, are much more like their true parents than their adoptive parents. This is true even of criminality; the criminality of the child is related to that of his true parents, whom he has never met, not of his adoptive parents, who are in constant contact with him. Adopted children thus provide very strong additional evidence for the importance of genetic factors in producing differences in personality; taken together with the twin studies, they clinch the case. This conclusion may sound strange to readers brought up at a time when the *zeitgeist* is strongly environmentalist and when the Freudian teachings about the importance of the first five years in the development of the child's personality are widely accepted. So, let us remember, were theories about the flat earth or the circling of the sun around the earth; the fact that the *zeitgeist* favours certain theories does not provide evidence for their correctness. If we look impartially at the evidence for the Freudian notions, or those related to environmentalism, we shall find little that is scientifically acceptable. It is nothing short of tragic that so many mothers (and perhaps fathers too) worry about the bringing up of their children and blame themselves for anything that seems to have gone wrong, as if their actions in looking after their children were primarily responsible for their character and their abilities and achievements. The truth, of course, is simply that the influence of parents is strictly limited; their major contribution to the future of their child is made when they join their chromosomes and shuffle their genes into the unique pattern that will for ever after determine the looks, the behaviour, the personality and the intellect of the child. How much more relaxed the parents could be if only they realized the limitations which nature has put on their later contributions !

We have now arrived at a rudimentary model of personality. We measure groups of traits, each trait being measured by a set of questions (thirty each in the questionnaires contained in this book). The traits in each group hang together to define a type, and we have altogether three such types. Neither traits nor types are right or wrong, good or bad; there are good and bad points about each one of them. Extreme traits or types present difficulties, but these need not be insuperable. A person's character and temperament are laid down by his genetic endowment; environment interacts with this, but in the ordinary course of events cannot do very much to change it. (This does not rule out the possibility that quite unusual circumstances might produce gross changes; thus the experience of having been an inmate in a concentration camp may have considerable and life-long consequences. We are here talking about more mundane experiences, such as might occur in most people's lives.) What is inherited does not necessarily make us like our parents, it may rather make us unlike them; the processes involved in hereditary determination are quite complex.

Many readers will at this point wish to voice a number of criticisms, or at least questions. They may say, for instance, that questionnaires seem very liable to certain distortions which might completely erode their usefulness. One obvious problem is the subjectivity of the questions. When asked whether he has many headaches, a person may reasonably reply: 'How many is many? How severe does a headache have to be in order to count? Sometimes I go for a long time without one, then I have a lot, one after the other. How do I count that?' In other words, we may seem to be asking for a comparison of his own experience with that of others, without spelling out what the experience of others really is. As a source of objective, quantitative information, the question clearly leaves much to be desired. How can we hope to get any sensible and useful information from such biased material?

The answer is that the subjectivity of the question is intentional. It is possible that an emotionally unstable person has in fact more headaches than a stable person. It is also possible that he has the same number, but notices them more because of the strong emotions which he experiences as a consequence. Or else an emotionally unstable person may like to seek attention by complaining a lot about his health. Our question would catch all these different causes of a 'Yes' answer; this would be much more useful than specifying that three headaches, of at least moderate severity, constituted 'many'. Such a specification would not catch the subjective, emotional reactions that it is our main purpose to capture.

There is a certain aura of subjectivity about this. Fortunately we have two objective criteria to check our hypotheses. The first of these we have already encountered: a given item must correlate positively with other items measuring the same thing. If our headache item succeeds in doing that, it is *eo ipso* a good item. This is an internal criterion (that is, internal to the construction of the scale or questionnaire). But we may prefer an outside criterion, or indeed we may prefer to rely only on combinations of inside and outside criteria. Such an outside criterion would be the difference in answer patterns observed in comparing a normal and a neurotic population. It is known that the neurotic group is characterized by emotional instability; if our item measures this tendency, then the neurotic group should endorse it significantly more often than a control, normal group which would be on the whole less unstable. If the item passes this test also, then we may accept it. We cannot argue that it gives us veridical information, that neurotics or emotionally unstable people do in fact have more headaches than stable people (although special research has shown that this is so); but we can conclude that unstable people more frequently say 'Yes' to the question. For the purpose of personality diagnosis, this is sufficient.

1	Do you have dizzy turns?	Yes	No
2	Do you get palpitations or thumping in your heart?	Yes	No
3	Did you ever have a nervous breakdown?	Yes	No
4	Have you ever been off work through sickness a good deal?	Yes	No
5	Did you often use to get 'stage fright' in your life?	Yes	No
6	Do you find it difficult to get into conversation with strangers?	Yes	No
7	Have you ever been troubled by a stammer or stutter?	Yes	No
8	Have you ever been made unconscious for two hours or more by an accident or blow?	Yes	No
9	Do you worry too long over humiliating experiences?	Yes	No
10	Do you consider yourself rather a nervous person?	Yes	No
11	Are your feelings easily hurt?	Yes	No
12	Do you usually keep in the background on social occasions?	Yes	No
13	Are you subject to attacks of shaking or trembling?	Yes	No
14	Are you an irritable person?	Yes	No
15	Do ideas run through your head so that you cannot sleep?	Yes	No
16	Do you worry over possible misfortunes?	Yes	No
17	Are you rather shy?	Yes	No
18	Do you sometimes feel happy, sometimes depressed, without any apparent reason?	Yes	No

19	Do you daydream a lot?	Yes	No
20	Do you seem to have less life about you than others?	Yes	No
21	Do you sometimes get a pain over your heart?	Yes	No
22	Do you have nightmares?	Yes	No
23	Do you worry about your health?	Yes	No
24	Have you sometimes walked in your sleep?	Yes	No
25	Do you sweat a great deal without exercise?	Yes	No
26	Do you find it difficult to make friends?	Yes	No
27	Does your mind often wander badly, so that you lose track of what you are doing?	Yes	No
28	Are you touchy on various subjects?	Yes	No
29	Do you often feel disgruntled?	Yes	No
30	Do you often feel just miserable?	Yes	No
31	Do you often feel self-conscious in the presence of superiors?	Yes	No
32	Do you suffer from sleeplessness?	Yes	No
33	Did you ever get short of breath without having done heavy work?	Yes	No
34	Do you ever suffer from severe headaches?	Yes	No
35	Do you suffer from 'nerves'?	Yes	No
36	Are you troubled by aches and pains?	Yes	No
37	Do you get nervous in places such as lifts, trains or tunnels?	Yes	No
38	Do you suffer from attacks of diarrhoea?	Yes	No
39	Do you lack self confidence?	Yes	No
40	Are you troubled with feelings of inferiority?	Yes	No

Let us study an example of this method of proof which reports actual data. Consider the questionnaire printed above; it consists of forty questions, all of them theoretically related to the concept of emotional instability. (Question 34 deals with headaches, although it is worded slightly differently.) These questions all correlate together, so that the internal criterion for a questionnaire is fulfilled. What would happen if we administered the questionnaire to 1,000 normal and 1,000 neurotic males, of equal age and educational experience? The score is simply the number of 'Yes' answers; it is found that on the average the normals give 9.98 'Yes' answers, the neurotics 20.01. Figure 6 shows the distribution of scores of the two groups; it will be seen that 145 of the neurotics have scores of 30 or above, while only one solitary normal has a score that high! Of the neurotics, 144 have scores from 27 to 29; only 12 normals are in this range. Another 124 neurotics score between 24 and 26, but only 21 normals. These are very large differences; they give us some confidence in the validity of the questionnaire.

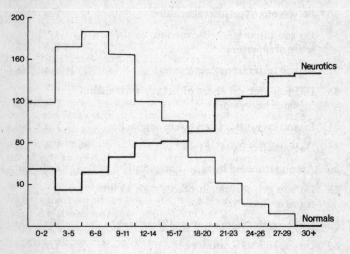

Figure 6

A proper analysis would look at each item, rather than only at the total score on the questionnaire. Figure 7 shows the percentage endorsements of neurotics and normals for sixteen selected questions in the questionnaire. In each case, it will be

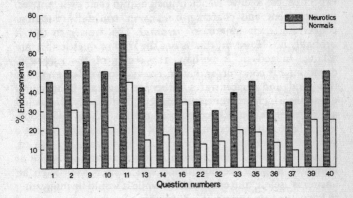

Figure 7

seen, the neurotics show a much higher proportion of 'Yes' answers; usually the neurotics have a score over twice that produced by the normals. It may be asked why the differentiation is not complete; why is there any overlap at all? There are many answers to that, including the obvious one that all measuring instruments are imperfect, but some are more imperfect than others ! The real point is that any so-called 'normal' population is so only by default in many cases; if a psychiatrist were to interview each member of such an apparently 'normal' group extensively, he would diagnose a proportion of them as being in need of psychiatric help, the exact proportion depending on the sample, the psychiatrist and many other factors. Thus the groups probably overlap in fact; the separation is imperfect and this is reflected in the scores on the questionnaire. Had we achieved perfect separation, we would have demonstrated beyond any question that either we had cheated, or the questionnaire was not measuring what it was supposed to be measuring ! The result achieved, namely a

good but imperfect separation of the groups, is all that could
have been expected and suffices as proof of the validity of the
questionnaire.

Another criticism is probably more valid. Can we really
expect people to have sufficient insight into their own motives,
temperament and character to answer truthfully questions
concerning their innermost *persona*? The answer to this is
probably no. However, that is not the kind of question we are
asking; indeed, it is perhaps the secret of the successful
questionnaire constructor that he manages to avoid questions of
this kind and concentrates rather on factual, behavioural
questions which everyone can answer quite readily. He would
ask questions about liking to go to parties, which few people
would have difficulties with, but not questions about having a
good sense of humour. Experience has shown that when you ask
a question like 'Do you have a better-than-average sense of
humour?' 95% of the population will answer 'Yes!' Such an
answer is useless, and consequently while it would be interesting
to know the true answer, it is clear that a questionnaire cannot
supply it. There are other ways of getting at it, however, and for
the sake of a demonstration we have included in this book a
typical 'sense of humour test'. The main point, however, is that
each question is carefully considered from this point of
view—does it call for insight on the part of the testee, to an
extent that is unreasonable to expect? Even if the answer to this
question is no, we would of course still insist on trying it out first
and showing that it passed both the internal and the external
criteria, as described above, before including it in our
questionnaire. There are many questions we would have liked to
ask, but had to exclude for these reasons; this is undoubtedly a
weakness in the questionnaire, but not an insurmountable one.

Even if people know the true answer to a question, they may
be unwilling to tell you. 'Faking good' and malingering are two
great obstacles in the way of gaining an insight into personality
by way of questionnaire (or interview!) and there is no doubt
that under suitable circumstances people will adopt these
methods for their own purposes. There is ample evidence that
they can, and do, falsify their answers when they feel that
something is to be gained by it. In some experiments, applicants

for certain posts were given questionnaires, half before being accepted, half after having been accepted. Those who had been accepted scored much higher on questions and traits which one would have considered less socially acceptable and desirable; in other words, they were more honest than those who thought that their answers would count towards their being offered the job.

Thus, where people are being selected, we may expect them to dissimulate in order to impress the prospective employer; there are ways of meeting this challenge, for example by the construction of 'Lie' scales (questionnaires which measure propensity to lie under these circumstances) but this is not the place to enter into a description of such devices. In ordinary experimental circumstances, people are only too willing to play ball and give honest answers; in fact, we have always been surprised (and impressed) by the truthfulness shown by the subjects of our investigations. This is, of course, even more true when a patient or client comes for treatment; he is highly motivated to be truthful, because he realizes that the success of the treatment may depend on his giving an accurate picture of himself.

How can we tell whether people tell the truth or not? One simple way is the following. Collect together a number of 'judges', that is, people who consent to choose from among their friends one or two extreme extraverts, and one or two extreme introverts. (The meaning of these terms is, of course, carefully explained to them.) The friends so chosen are then given the questionnaire, and their scores computed. If they are giving an accurate picture of themselves, then they should score pretty much in the way the original judges (who after all knew them well) had predicted. This in fact is how the experiment turns out; the questionnaire responses agree very well indeed with the ratings made by the 'judges'. In other words, people's behaviour is congruent with what they say their habitual behaviour is. It is only under conditions where telling lies is obviously to their advantage that they depart from truthfulness. In fact, people seem to enjoy filling in questionnaires concerning their own personality. We have often found that when questionnaires are distributed in a school or university, or place of work, those absent at the time contact us full of wrath, asking why they have been omitted and demanding to be allowed to fill in the questionnaire all the same! A series of well-chosen questions is rightly regarded as a challenge to know oneself better, and for most people this is a desirable end in itself. In these groups there is also always a strong desire to be given the results of the study; they want to know just how they come out, in comparison with the rest. This too is understandable; it is only by comparing ourselves with others that we can get some idea of our relative position in the group. Many people are quite compulsive about telling the truth, the whole truth, and nothing but the truth; they will not only fill in the questionnaire, but write long postscripts to explain precisely how they interpreted certain questions and the reasons why they said 'Yes' or 'No'.

In a book like this, of course, falsification is probably not a serious problem. After all, the only person who needs to know your answers is yourself; to cheat yourself is like cheating at patience — it is pointless. Even if you do, no great harm is done. But if you have a close friend, or relative, or marriage partner, you might like to go through your answers with them — you may be interested in how others see you, even with respect to very obvious behaviour patterns which you might think would be obvious to everybody! In fact, it may be interesting to draw up a second personality profile for yourself, based on your friend's replies, and compare this with your own; this is a rough way of comparing your personality as it really is with the picture of it as it may appear to the outside observer. In some regions, such as extraversion-introversion, the correspondence is likely to be very close; in others, such as emotional instability, it may not be. This is very much an inner feeling which may be kept under tight control, so that even good friends may not see any evidence of the inner turmoil. In any case, the exercise is useful, and may be amusing; it may also lead to a mending of your fences as far as the picture you present to the outer world is concerned. (You would, of course, want to buy a second copy of the book for this purpose!)

We have mentioned in passing several ways in which a questionnaire can be shown to be valid, that is, to measure what it is supposed to be measuring. There are other ways of showing that, and the most powerful method widely used is that of the

miniature situation test. What is done here is quite simply to
construct a laboratory test in which the subject is asked to
perform certain actions which are relevant to the measurement
of a trait which has already been measured by means of a
questionnaire; the interest centres on the correlation between
his answers to the questionnaire and his actual performance.
Let us suppose that the trait we are interested in is that of
persistence, and that we have constructed a persistence
questionnaire which we wish to validate. How would we set
about making up miniature situations suitable for measuring
persistence?

One way might be to administer an intelligence test to our
subjects, made up of fairly easy questions, and also of a few very
difficult ones — so difficult, in fact, that they are for all intents
and purposes insoluble for the people involved. We could then
time their efforts to solve these problems, and see whether they
give up easily, or persist for a long time. The score would be the
number of minutes spent on trying to solve the insoluble
problems. Or again, along quite different lines, we might give
our subjects a dynamometer; this is an instrument in which you
press a handle against a spring, and the strength of your grip is
shown on a clock-face by means of a moving indicator. Subjects
are instructed to press as hard as they can; they are then
instructed to keep on pressing at half their maximum strength
(as shown on the clock-face) for as long as they can. Having thus
eliminated differences in brute strength, this test becomes one
of persistence; again, the score is the number of minutes the
subject keeps on pressing. Odd as it may seem, persistence on
these two tests (and many others which have been constructed)
shows a reasonable correlation, establishing that they measure
the same underlying trait. We can now correlate the results of
our whole battery of tests with our questionnaire and obtain
evidence for or against our hypothesis that the questionnaire is a
good measure of persistence. We would, of course, also obtain
whatever other evidence was obtainable, such as ratings of the
persistence of our subjects from teachers, employers, or whoever
might know reasonably well how our subjects behaved at school
or work.

Yet another method may be used for the purpose of

validation, this time combining theory and laboratory experiment. We shall only give a brief account of this method as we do not want to turn this brief introduction into a text-book. Consider our questionnaire on sexual attitudes and behaviour, given later in this book. This contains several questions regarding the search for novelty; search for new partners, for new positions in intercourse, for new experiences. We have found that extraverts in particular score highly on questions of this kind; they get quickly bored with their partners, and search for new fields to conquer. Why is this so — or is it only a verbal report, without substance? How can we support our belief that these accounts are truthful, meaningful and valid?

Theory tells us that this changeable behaviour may have something to do with a psychological and physiological process called *habituation*. If you sit quietly in a room, and someone suddenly sounds off a raucous claxon near your ear, this will cause you to jump and to show a whole number of physiological changes — your heart will beat faster, your palms will begin to sweat, your breathing will go faster, etcetera. If now this claxon is sounded repeatedly, your reactions will become much less extreme; they will habituate so much that after twenty or thirty soundings you will hardly react at all. Now extraverts have been found to habituate much more quickly than introverts; there are physiological reasons for this which we cannot enter into here. (Interested readers will find a non-technical account in H.J. Eysenck's Pelican on *Fact and Fiction in Psychology*.) Here we may have found the explanation for the conduct of our extraverts in seeking variety in the sexual field — and in others as well; extraverts move house more frequently, change jobs more frequently, show less 'brand loyalty' in their shopping habits, and are in every way more changeable.

It is possible to put these hypotheses together and check them in the experimental laboratory. Dr E. Nelson showed 'blue' films to groups of extraverts and introverts (one person at a time of course!) There were nine such films, carefully edited so that each film consisted of different snippets showing just one kind of sexual behaviour — it might be kissing and cuddling, front-to-front intercourse, orgies, or whatever. Each film lasted for four minutes and on each of three separate days three films were shown, with four minutes elapsing between films. Physiological reactions of the subjects were monitored, including a measure of their penile reactions (it is quite easy to measure the amount of erection shown by the penis). It was predicted and found that extraverts showed the phenomenon of habituation during the showing of each film, from film to film, and from occasion to occasion; in other words, their erection showed progressive lessening from the peak value obtained at the beginning of the first film. Introverts did not habituate at all. We can thus create a meaningful theoretical web including extraversion, as measured by the questionnaire, the physiological phenomenon of habituation, and the physiological effects of habituation in the sexual field. It is by the construction of such *nomological networks*, as the philosophers of science call them, that this method of proof proceeds.

In addition to the direct approaches to personality (as illustrated in our questionnaires on extraversion, emotional instability and toughmindedness) and the indirect approaches (as illustrated in our test of sense of humour) we have used specialized measures such as the test of sexual attitudes and behaviour, mentioned above. The reason for this is that sex plays such an important part in our lives and that sexual attitudes and behaviours, while linked fairly closely with the major factors of personality, are nevertheless something rather different and deserve special consideration. Analysis of the answers to our questions, along the statistical lines of correlational analysis, revealed the existence of a number of reaction patterns such as permissiveness, liking for impersonal sex, sexual shyness, aggressive sex, sexual disgust, liking for physical sex, and so forth. These, as in the case of personality traits, were not uncorrelated and gave rise to two major sexual 'types' (using the term again in the modern sense). The first of these is the libidinal type, characterised by a liking for impersonal sex, for pornography, permissive, always on the look-out for physical sex and sexual excitement, lacking entirely in shyness, disgust and prudishness. As might have been expected, this type is much more frequently found in extraverts, particularly when these are also toughminded. It is also found more frequently in males than in females—so much so that we have had to prepare separate scoring keys for the two sexes.

The second major factor in this field is satisfaction; oddly enough, sexual satisfaction (that is, satisfaction with one's own sex life) is entirely independent from the first factor, libidinal strength. It is possible to be satisfied with one's sex life regardless of the strength of one's libido; strong sexual urges, impersonal and permissive sexual behaviour, do not seem to cause greater or lesser satisfaction than weak sexual urges, stress on personal relations and restrictive sexual behaviour. This fact may upset both the libertines and the puritans; nevertheless, that is how the results come out. Perhaps all that the result shows is that extraverts and introverts both have their own definition of a happy life and reach it by different routes; it is somewhat absurd to specify for others how they should reach their particular heaven! Indeed, this is a lesson which readers should take to heart in the most general way; the fact that their particular style of life is satisfactory for them does not mean that it would be so for everybody else. Individual differences are strong and far-reaching; they are securely anchored in innate physiological structures which determine a person's reactions to environmental stimulation of all kinds. We should value and understand these individual differences and not press for uniformity which would only result in suppressing an important part of society.

There is one further set of questions we have included in this book. This deals with social and political attitudes and readers may wonder what these have to do with personality. The obvious answer of course is that attitudes, whether social, political or sexual, form an important aspect of personality; we have already shown that certain sexual attitudes and behaviours are intimately linked with certain personality types, and the same is found in the case of social and political attitudes. Again we have a series of primary attitudes, such as ethnocentrism or racism, pacifism, religionism (a rather horrible neologism to denote belief in religious values), libertarianism, socialism and so forth. These are correlated, and fall into a pattern made up of two major social attitude factors, one of which is the well-known radicalism-conservatism scale, of which Gilbert and Sullivan used to sing how comical it is that 'Nature always does contrive, that every boy and every gal that's born into this world alive, is either a little liberal, or else a little conservative.' The rhyme may be dubious, but the sentiment only too true. The right and the left in politics have played their part for many years, and may do so for many years to come.

However, it would be quite wrong to imagine that this dimension or continuum is the only one that is relevant in this field; equally important is another one which we have called toughmindedness *v* tendermindedness. The fact that these terms are identical with those used for our major personality dimensions is not accidental, of course; there is strong evidence that toughminded people (in the sense of having that sort of personality) hold toughminded attitudes! The precise nature of this factor will become apparent when readers answer the questions in the attitude questionnaire. However, it may be useful to hint at the nature of this dimension by recalling Koestler's book *The Yogi and the Commissar*. The commissar is the toughminded, the Yogi the tenderminded one. Unlikely as it may seem, these major attitude patterns are in good part mediated by genetic causes (presumably working through personality factors). It is this discovery, in part, which caused us to include this particular inventory; the genetic connection with personality seemed to indicate a much closer relationship than had been envisaged previously.

It may be asked what the purpose is of such attitude questionnaires; most people surely know already whether they vote Conservative or Labour? That is quite true, but there are many oddities about voting behaviour and social attitudes. Thus for instance the Labour Party is supposed to be the progressive, radical party; yet it is supported in the main by working-class folk whose attitudes tend to be very conservative. It will be remembered how the dockers marched to the Houses of Parliament in support of Enoch Powell and his very non-progressive policies regarding coloured immigration. There are many other similar examples. Middle-class people, even though tending to vote for the Conservative Party, tend to be more progressive than working-class people. There is much evidence along these lines, both from work done in this country and also in the United States; it has been described in detail in H. J. Eysenck's *Psychology Is About People*. It is this curious

paradox that the 'progressive' and 'radical' party is supported by
the more conservative sections of the population, while the
'Conservatives' are in the main supported by the more radical
sections of the population, which makes detailed measurement
of social attitudes so interesting, going well beyond simple party
adherence.

One further psychological finding may be mentioned here, in
case the reader finds himself at one extreme or the other of the
attitude scales here included. Many years ago, R. H. Thouless
enunciated his 'law of certainty', based on a large body of
research. It reads as follows: 'When, in a group of persons, there
are influences acting both in the direction of acceptance and of
rejection of a belief, the result is not to make the majority adopt
a lower degree of conviction, but to make some hold the belief
with a high degree of conviction, while others reject it also with a
high degree of conviction.' In other words, when nobody knows
with any certainty what the truth is, people adopt extreme
positions, either for or against. On most of the social issues
mentioned in the questions of the social attitude questionnaire
the truth is not known; if therefore a person has extreme scores,
he is likely to have adopted his stance for emotional, not for
rational reasons. It might be wise for him to consider whether
there might not be some sense also in the arguments of the
opposing side!

This completes our brief survey of the inventories included,
and the reasons for considering questionnaires of this kind
reliable and valid measuring instruments — at least for certain
purposes. We must next turn to a consideration of the way the
results are to be interpreted and the use to which they can be put
by the reader. We have already explained that scores on
questionnaires acquire meaning only by comparison with scores
obtained by other people; it would be meaningless to talk of
Robinson Crusoe's extraversion or introversion! Similarly, a
person is tall or short only by comparison with others. Thus
above all a questionnaire needs to be administered to large and
hopefully representative samples of the population; it is by
comparing himself with the distribution of scores obtained from
such a population that the reader can acquire some sense of
belongingness.

Actually, most published questionnaires fall down rather badly on the job of providing a proper standardization group. As personality differs in males and females and also by age, very large groups have to be tested and separate norms provided for the two sexes and different ages. Many questionnaires intended for serious clinical and experimental work fail to provide such separate norms; some even use only student groups for their standardization. To give an indication of the size of the job that is required, let us just mention that in standardizing the Eysenck Personality Questionnaire, which was designed for serious clinical and experimental work, and on which much of this book is based, over 12,000 males and females, adults and children, normals, neurotics, criminals and psychotics were tested, as well as 2,000 pairs of twins — plus another large number of adults and children used in preparing earlier versions of the scales, versions which never saw the light of publication.

The requirements of professionally useful questionnaires are of course much heavier than those for a book of this kind which does not aim to give precise measurements, but rather aims to give a general indication of the personality profiles that are characteristic of individual readers. It must be emphasized that if personality investigations are required for clinical or occupational or educational reasons, readers should have the job done professionally, by a clinical, occupational or educational psychologist. He would be able to take into account niceties such as sex and age differences which we have purposely neglected for the most part. He would also be able to explain in greater detail the meaning of the resulting profile, and its implications for future action. No book can do this properly, because so much depends on the actual circumstances of the person in question. Hence this book is suggested for use only in the sense that it may provide some increase in self-knowledge, some insight, and perhaps some amusement. It is not meant to serve any more serious purpose.

The items used for our scales come from literally hundreds of different published and unpublished scales and investigations, and the selection of traits used for the various scales was very much determined by work published by others over the years, as well as by our own studies. For some of the scales published here we have had proper population samples, obtained for us by commercial firms specializing in Gallup-poll-type investigations; for other scales we have drawn on smaller populations used on various occasions. Fortunately social class plays little part in affecting personality—unlike intelligence, where classification by social class is absolutely essential, as otherwise the results would be completely meaningless. Several of the studies on which we have relied are being written up for publication in books or journals; others have already been published. There would be no point in detailing the samples used, and the methods employed, for each of the questionnaires here printed; this would take up many pages, and have little meaning for most readers. Let us merely state that for reasons given, no great accuracy is claimed for individual scores; readers will get a valid overall impression of their personality profiles, but for precise measurement they must consult expert testers for individual testing. The position here is very much like that resulting from the publication of *Know Your Own IQ* and *Check Your Own IQ*—the results of self-testing are indicative, but not sufficiently accurate to base important decisions upon.

In actual fact, psychologists often disparage and discourage the publication of popular accounts of this kind, and in particular the publication of self-testing devices. The argument seems to be that in this way the mystique of psychological testing is torn to shreds and that knowledge of the results may do harm to certain individuals. The argument about mystique is hardly tenable; if a profession's reputation depends on keeping secret its methods, and preventing people from knowing the strengths and weaknesses of those methods, it is hardly worth preserving. The other argument may have greater substance, although we doubt it. There have been quite a number of cases of people measuring their own IQ on the basis of the Pelican books just mentioned, finding to their suprise that they were very much brighter than they thought and deciding to go on to further study or to University; we have had letters and messages of thanks from people who but for this revelation would not have gone on to worthwhile and successful careers, degrees and diplomas. We have not heard from a single person who felt that doing the tests and obtaining an estimate of his own IQ had in any way harmed him; knowing the habits of letter writers, who are always far more ready to criticize than to praise, we feel that this indicates that the good effects probably outweighed the bad — if any. We believe that the same will be true for this book also.

What possible advantages may a reader obtain from filling in the questionnaires and calculating his scores on the various tests? In the first place, he will obtain some indication of his personality pattern as compared with the majority; he will see graphically on which traits and type-scales he deviates to any marked extent from the average. Up and down in this case do not of course carry any pejorative or evaluative meaning; he may be above or below the average numerically, but neither indicates that he is in any sense better or worse than the majority — just somewhat different. To be aware of these differences is important; most people project their own personalities onto other people and believe that others are essentially very much like them. This is patently untrue and it is a valuable part of insight to realize that one is different, and in what way one is different, from other people. For some people, the opposite is true; they think that only they are characterized by certain strengths, weaknesses, or excesses, and they are either disappointed or reassured to find that many other people are in fact similar to them.

Recognition of one's own position on these various scales may alert one to look at other people (including one's spouse and one's children, one's friends and one's enemies) in a different way. It is perhaps not too much to say that contraries on these scales usually simply cannot understand each other; the typical introvert can get very annoyed and frustrated when confronted by the typical extravert — and vice versa. Neither can believe that another person could be so differently constituted, and both prefer to believe that the other behaves as he does 'because he knows it teases'. This of course is not so, but for a person who fundamentally believes that all other people are essentially very much like himself it may very well seem so. Going through the questionnaires included in this book may teach him to look at other people with a more impartial eye, and recognize their particular personalities more readily and objectively. Once you can identify someone as a typical extravert or a typical introvert, you are less likely to ask him to behave in ways which are contrary to his true personality; your expectations are more realistic, and less likely to be disappointed. This is a valuable gain, and while personality impressions are never likely to be a hundred per cent correct, even a reasonable increase in accuracy may be of importance in interpersonal relations.

This is particularly true of personal relations in marriage. There are two major fallacies about marriage current: one is that like marries like (homogamy) and the other that people marry spouses whose personality complements their own, that like marries unlike. Homogamy exists for intelligence; bright males marry bright females on the whole, and in fact the correspondence is quite close. But for personality, no rules exist at all; the correlations between husbands and wives for our various personality scales are all very low, around zero. (This is not true of the attitude measures, where homogamy obtains; attitudes of husbands and wives correlate about as highly as their IQs.) Thus there will be many cases where one marriage partner is extraverted, the other introverted; this produces many arguments and problems unless both realize their constitutional differences and attempt to take these into account in coming to a suitable *modus vivendi*. This may be difficult, but knowledge of the facts may be of great help.

What about emotional instability and maladjustment? Suppose we find ourselves in the position of having very high scores on the scales included under this heading; is there anything we can do? There are several pieces of advice which may be useful. The most obvious is to go to a doctor; he may refer the sufferer to a psychiatrist, and there are now many different ways and means of treating these troubles, for example, by means of behaviour therapy (described in H.J. Eysenck's Pelican, *Fact and Fiction in Psychology*). These methods are reasonably quick and efficacious, and involve neither drugs nor physical interference, such as electric shock or brain operations. It is unlikely that a person having such high scores would not be aware of his or her unhappy state; the objective scores may have the happy result of pushing them into doing something about their troubles. True, they have inherited a nervous system liable to strong and lasting emotional reactions, too strong for the types of stimuli evoking them, but the psychologist can sever the associative bonds which have tied these strong emotional reactions to certain special stimuli, and relieve the patient's trouble in this way. Neurotic disorders are very widespread and there is no reason for shame in being one of what amounts possibly to a third of the population. Keeping quiet about it is certainly no way to deal with it; active measures are called for.

This brings us to the end of our introduction; the various questionnaires follow. It may be worth while to recapitulate the main points. The purpose of the book is to give the reader insight into his own personality, and a model into which to fit other people, particularly his friends and enemies, his family, and other people whose behaviour may be important to him. The scores are suggestive rather than definitive; they are approximate, rather than precise and accurate. For any practical purpose, the reader would do well to go to a psychologist and have a more detailed measurement of his personality carried out; self-measurement cannot in the nature of the case give the same degree of precision as measurement carried out by an expert. Our comparison scores do not take into account such factors as age or sex (except in a few isolated instances where differences between the sexes were too large to make it meaningful to rest content with a joint figure). We have indicated roughly how the two sexes are differentiated and in looking at his or her scores, the reader may like to remember these broad guidelines. We have suggested a few ways in which the book may be useful but, above all, we hope that it will serve to amuse and stimulate the reader. If he goes on to visit his library and take out a few books on psychology, so much the better. 'The proper study of mankind is man,' and the more we learn about man, the better we will be able to cope with our fellow men.

2

EXTRAVERSION-INTROVERSION

The first of the three major typologies of temperament described in the last chapter is extraversion-introversion. This major area can in turn be broken down into at least seven component characteristics or 'sub-factors'. These will be described along with a method for scoring them and comparing yourself with other people after the questionnaire has been completed. Now work through the 210 questions given below putting a circle around the 'Yes' or the 'No'. If you find it impossible to decide one way or the other for any reason, put a ring around the '?'. If you prefer not to mark the book, so that other people can use it (and obviously this applies if you are borrowing the copy from a library), you can write on another piece of paper the question numbers and your answers to each of them. It is best if you work quickly and don't dwell too much on the exact wording of the questions. If some of them seem repetitive, remember that there are good reasons for getting at the same thing in slightly different ways.

Questionnaire

1   Are you happiest when you get involved in some project that calls for rapid action?   Yes   ?   No

2   Do you like going out a lot?   Yes   ?   No

3   Would you prefer a job involving change, travel and variety even though risky and insecure?   Yes   ?   No

4   Do you like planning things well ahead of time?   Yes   ?   No

5 Do you sit calmly when you are watching a race or competitive sport?   Yes ? No

6 Do you like to have time to be alone with your thoughts?   Yes ? No

7 Are you inclined to be overconscientious?   Yes ? No

8 Do you become restless when working at something in which there is little action?   Yes ? No

9 Do you often need understanding friends to cheer you up?   Yes ? No

10 Do you quite enjoy taking risks?   Yes ? No

11 Do you usually make up your mind quickly?   Yes ? No

12 If you are watching a slapstick film or farcical play do you laugh louder than most of the people around you?   Yes ? No

13 Do you frequently pause just to meditate about things in general?   Yes ? No

14 Are you normally on time for appointments?   Yes ? No

15 When climbing stairs do you usually take them two at a time?   Yes ? No

16 Generally, do you prefer reading to meeting people?   Yes ? No

17 Do you lock up your house carefully at night?   Yes ? No

18 Do you often change your interests?   Yes ? No

19 Is your anger quick and short?   Yes ? No

20 Do you often philosophize about the purpose of human existence?   Yes ? No

21 Do you live by the maxim that a job worth doing is worth doing well?   Yes ? No

22 When you are driving in a car, do you get
    very frustrated by slow-moving traffic?   Yes ? No

23 Are you fairly talkative when you are with
    a group of people?   Yes ? No

24 Do you think that young children should
    have to learn to cross roads by themselves?   Yes ? No

25 Before making up your mind, do you care-
    fully consider all the advantages and dis-
    advantages?   Yes ? No

26 Does a sentimental film easily move you to
    tears?   Yes ? No

27 Do you often try to find the underlying
    motives for the actions of other people?   Yes ? No

28 Can you always be fully relied upon?   Yes ? No

29 Are you inclined to be slow and deliberate
    in your actions?   Yes ? No

30 Can you usually let yourself go and have a
    good time at a party?   Yes ? No

31 When the odds are against you, do you still
    usually think it worth taking a chance?   Yes ? No

32 Do you often buy things on impulse?   Yes ? No

33 Are you able to maintain outer calm in the
    face of an emergency?   Yes ? No

34 Would you rather read the sports page
    than the editorial leaders in a newspaper?   Yes ? No

35 Are you inclined to live each day as it
    comes along?   Yes ? No

36 Do you usually finish your meals faster
    than other people even though there is no
    reason to hurry?   Yes ? No

37 Do you hate being with a crowd who play
    practical jokes on one another?   Yes ? No

38 When you are catching a train, do you
often arrive at the last minute?   Yes ? No

39 Do you know what you will be doing on
your next holiday?   Yes ? No

40 Do you get very upset when watching
documentaries about living conditions in
less fortunate countries?   Yes ? No

41 Do you seldom stop to analyse your own
thoughts and feelings?   Yes ? No

42 Do you often leave things to the last
minute?   Yes ? No

43 Do other people regard you as a very lively
person?   Yes ? No

44 Do you like talking to people so much that
you never miss a chance of talking to a
stranger?   Yes ? No

45 Would life with no danger in it be too dull
for you?   Yes ? No

46 Can you make decisions quickly?   Yes ? No

47 Would you say that your temper is well
controlled?   Yes ? No

48 Are you keen about learning things even
though they may have no relevance to your
everyday life?   Yes ? No

49 Do you have a tendency to 'let things slide'
occasionally?   Yes ? No

50 Are you always 'on the go' when not
actually sleeping?   Yes ? No

51 If you were making a business enquiry
would you rather write than discuss it on
the telephone?   Yes ? No

52   Do you save regularly?   Yes   ?   No

53   Do you often get into a jam because you do
     things without thinking?   Yes   ?   No

54   Are you so carried away by music that you
     are usually compelled to conduct or dance
     in time with it?   Yes   ?   No

55   Do you like to solve 'brain teasers'?   Yes   ?   No

56   Do you have difficulty applying yourself to
     work that requires sustained concentra-
     tion?   Yes   ?   No

57   Do you like organizing and initiating
     leisure-time activities?   Yes   ?   No

58   Do you enjoy spending long periods of
     time by yourself?   Yes   ?   No

59   Would you enjoy fast driving?   Yes   ?   No

60   Do you generally do and say things with-
     out stopping to think?   Yes   ?   No

61   Do you prefer early classical music to
     swinging jazz?   Yes   ?   No

62   Do you frequently become so involved
     with a question or problem that you have
     to keep thinking about it until you arrive
     at a satisfactory solution?   Yes   ?   No

63   Does it often take you a long time to get
     started on something?   Yes   ?   No

64   Are you generally very enthusiastic about
     starting a new project or undertaking?   Yes   ?   No

65   Are you relaxed and self-confident in the
     company of other people?   Yes   ?   No

66   Would you make quite sure you had
     another job before giving up your old one?   Yes   ?   No

67 Do you usually think carefully before doing anything?   Yes ? No

68 Do you like to play pranks on other people?   Yes ? No

69 If you have been to see a play or film do you like to go over it in your mind for a long time afterwards?   Yes ? No

70 Do you often forget little things that you are supposed to do?   Yes ? No

71 When you are walking with other people do they often have difficulty keeping up with you?   Yes ? No

72 Are you more distant and reserved than most people?   Yes ? No

73 Do people who drive carefully annoy you?   Yes ? No

74 Would you rather plan things than do things?   Yes ? No

75 Do you subscribe to the philosophy of 'Eat drink, and be merry for tomorrow we die'?   Yes ? No

76 Are you frequently so lost in thought that you do not notice what is going on around you?   Yes ? No

77 Are you ordinarily a carefree person?   Yes ? No

78 At work or at play, do other people find it hard to keep up with the pace you set?   Yes ? No

79 Do you like mixing with lots of other people?   Yes ? No

80 Are you rather cautious in novel situations?   Yes ? No

81 Are you an impulsive person?   Yes ? No

82 Do you tell your friends what you think is wrong with them?   Yes ? No

83 Do you ever walk across the street against a
    red light?   Yes ? No

84 Would you enjoy writing a critical discuss-
    ion of a book or article?   Yes ? No

85 Are you inclined to rush from one activity
    to another without pausing for rest?   Yes ? No

86 Do you easily make new friends with mem-
    bers of your own sex?   Yes ? No

87 Would you do almost anything for a dare?   Yes ? No

88 Do you prefer activities that just happen to
    those planned in advance?   Yes ? No

89 If you were visiting Rio de Janeiro during
    carnival time would you rather observe
    the festivities than participate in them?   Yes ? No

90 Do you react to new ideas that you come
    across by analysing them to see how they
    fit in with your own point of view?   Yes ? No

91 Would you say that generally you have a
    serious and responsible attitude toward
    the world?   Yes ? No

92 Do you often find yourself hurrying to get
    to places even when there is plenty of time?   Yes ? No

93 Do you like to tell jokes and stories to
    groups of friends?   Yes ? No

94 When buying things, do you usually exa-
    mine the guarantee?   Yes ? No

95 When you meet new people, do you very
    quickly decide whether you like them or
    not?   Yes ? No

96 Are you usually among the last to stop
    clapping after the end of a concert or stage
    performance?   Yes ? No

97 Have you ever tried to write poetry?   Yes ? No

98 Are you considered an easy-going person?   Yes ? No

99 Are you frequently lacking in energy and
motivation to do things?   Yes ? No

100 Do you enjoy talking and playing with
young children?   Yes ? No

101 Do you think people spend too much time
safeguarding their future with savings and
insurances?   Yes ? No

102 Do you often do things on the spur of the
moment?   Yes ? No

103 Do you find it easy to discuss intimate and
personal matters with other members of
your family?   Yes ? No

104 Would you enjoy working on a project that
involved a great deal of library research?   Yes ? No

105 If you say you will do something do you
always keep your promise no matter how
inconvenient it might turn out to be?   Yes ? No

106 Do you like to lie in bed late in the week-
ends?   Yes ? No

107 Are you apprehensive about going into a
room full of strange people?   Yes ? No

108 Do you go in for regular health checks?   Yes ? No

109 If it were practically possible would you
like to live each day as it comes along?   Yes ? No

110 Have you ever been involved as a perform-
er in amateur dramatics or musical groups?   Yes ? No

111 Do you read a newspaper regularly?   Yes ? No

112 Do you sometimes have a tendency to be
'slap dash' in your work?   Yes ? No

113 Do you prefer holidays that are quiet and restful without a great deal of rushing about?   Yes ? No

114 Have you ever seriously felt you might be happier living by yourself on a desert island?   Yes ? No

115 Do you always wear a safety belt when travelling in a car?   Yes ? No

116 Do you like doing things in which you have to act quickly?   Yes ? No

117 Would you refrain from expressing your attitudes and opinions if you thought that others present might be offended by them?   Yes ? No

118 Do you enjoy solving problems even though they have no practical application?   Yes ? No

119 Do you usually answer a personal letter immediately after you have received it?   Yes ? No

120 Do you generally move about at a leisurely pace?   Yes ? No

121 Do you sometimes feel uncomfortable when people get too close to you physically?   Yes ? No

122 Do you sometimes gamble money on races, elections or such-like?   Yes ? No

123 Do you often get involved in things you later prefer to opt out of?   Yes ? No

124 Do you choose your words very carefully when discussing business matters?   Yes ? No

125 Are you so thoughtful and reflective that your friends sometimes call you a dreamer?   Yes ? No

126 Are you generally unconcerned about the future?   Yes ? No

127 When you wake up in the morning are you usually ready to 'get cracking'?   Yes ? No

128 Is it important to you to be liked by a wide range of people?   Yes ? No

129 Would you agree that an element of risk adds spice to life?   Yes ? No

130 Are you an easy-going person, not generally bothered about having everything 'just so'?   Yes ? No

131 When you are angry with someone do you wait until you have cooled off before tackling them about the incident?   Yes ? No

132 Are you overcome by a sense of wonder and excitement when visiting historical monuments?   Yes ? No

133 Can you honestly say that you honour your commitments more than most people?   Yes ? No

134 Are you usually full of pep and vigour?   Yes ? No

135 Do you spontaneously introduce yourself to strangers at social gatherings?   Yes ? No

136 Do you agree that one should 'neither a borrower nor a lender be'?   Yes ? No

137 When you go on a trip do you like to plan routes and timetables carefully?   Yes ? No

138 Can you keep an exciting secret for a long period of time?   Yes ? No

139 Do you frequently discuss the causes and possible solutions of social and political problems with your friends?   Yes ? No

140 Do you set an alarm clock if you have to be
up at a particular time in the morning   Yes ? No

141 Do you often feel tired and listless?   Yes ? No

142 Would you rather spend an evening talking to one interesting member of your own
sex than singing and dancing with a large
crowd of friends?   Yes ? No

143 Would being in debt worry you?   Yes ? No

144 Do you mostly speak before thinking
things out?   Yes ? No

145 Do you get so excited that you gesticulate
when you talk?   Yes ? No

146 Do you often spend an evening just read-
ing a book?   Yes ? No

147 Do you always follow the rule 'business before pleasure'?   Yes ? No

148 Do you like to have a lot of things to do all
the time?   Yes ? No

149 Do you like to be in the middle of things
socially speaking?   Yes ? No

150 Do you find that you have often crossed a
road leaving your more careful compan-
ions on the other side?   Yes ? No

151 Do you think an evening out is more successful if it is arranged at the last moment?   Yes ? No

152 If somebody expresses an opinion with
which you disagree do you tell them so
immediately?   Yes ? No

153 Would you rather see a comedy than a
documentary on TV?   Yes ? No

154 Do you often not bother to cast your vote
in an election?   Yes ? No

155 Do other people seem to get more done in
a day than you?   Yes   ?   No

156 Do you enjoy solitary activities such as
playing patience and solving cross-word
puzzles?   Yes   ?   No

157 Do you think the risk of lung cancer from
smoking has been exaggerated?   Yes   ?   No

158 Do you get so 'carried away' by new and
exciting ideas that you never think of the
possible snags?   Yes   ?   No

159 Would you find it impossible to make a
speech 'off the cuff'?   Yes   ?   No

160 Do you think it is pointless to analyse your
own value system and morality?   Yes   ?   No

161 Did you occasionally play truant in your
school days?   Yes   ?   No

162 Most days, are there times when you enjoy
just sitting and doing nothing?   Yes   ?   No

163 Are you inclined to avoid people whenever
possible?   Yes   ?   No

164 Would you always read the small print before signing a contract?   Yes   ?   No

165 Do you prefer to 'sleep on it' before making decisions?   Yes   ?   No

166 Are you given to making outrageous
threats even though you have no intention
of carrying them out?   Yes   ?   No

167 Do you enjoy essays on serious, philosophical subjects?   Yes   ?   No

168 Do you sometimes drink alcohol till you
reach a state of intoxication?   Yes   ?   No

169 Would you rather watch sports than play them?   Yes ? No

170 Would you be very unhappy if you were prevented from making numerous social contacts?   Yes ? No

171 When travelling in an aeroplane, bus or train, do you choose your seat with safety in mind?   Yes ? No

172 Do you prefer work that needs close attention most of the time?   Yes ? No

173 Do you wish that you were able to 'let yourself go' and have a good time more often?   Yes ? No

174 Do you think it a waste of time to formulate plans for an ideal society or Utopia?   Yes ? No

175 Would you go out of your way to find a rubbish bin rather than throw a wrapper on the street?   Yes ? No

176 Do you frequently take a nap in the middle of the day?   Yes ? No

177 Do you usually prefer to take your recreation with companions rather than alone?   Yes ? No

178 Are you careful to swim between the lifesaver's flags at the beach?   Yes ? No

179 Do you need to use a lot of self-control to keep out of trouble?   Yes ? No

180 Are you hesitant to ask strangers for a street direction?   Yes ? No

181 Are you bored by discussions of what life might be like in the future?   Yes ? No

182 Do you have regular dental check-ups?   Yes ? No

183 Do you get agitated if you have to wait for someone?   Yes ? No

184 Do you like to have many social engage-
   ments?   Yes ? No

185 Do you avoid 'thrill' rides such as roller-
   coasters and ferris wheels when at an
   amusement park?   Yes ? No

186 When you want to buy something expen-
   sive can you save up for some time patient-
   ly?   Yes ? No

187 Are you likely to swear loudly if you trip
   over something or hit your finger with a
   hammer?   Yes ? No

188 Do you like work that involves action
   rather than profound thought and study?   Yes ? No

189 Have you occasionally 'played sick' to
   avoid an unpleasant responsibility?   Yes ? No

190 If you think you may have to wait a few
   minutes for a lift are you inclined to take
   the stairs instead?   Yes ? No

191 Do you enjoy entertaining people?   Yes ? No

192 Would you always be careful to declare
   everything at the customs if you had tra-
   velled abroad?   Yes ? No

193 Would you agree that planning things
   ahead takes the fun out of life?   Yes ? No

194 Are you prone to exaggeration and elabor-
   ation when relating a story to your friends? Yes ? No

195 Are you bored by museums that feature
   archaeology and classical history?   Yes ? No

196 Do you think it is pointless to make provi-
   sion for your old age?   Yes ? No

197 Normally, do you tend to do things at a
   rapid rate?   Yes ? No

198 Are you inclined to limit your acquaintances to a select few?   Yes ? No

199 Do you arrive at appointments with plenty of time to spare?   Yes ? No

200 Do you hate standing in a long queue for anything?   Yes ? No

201 Do you like highly coloured modern paintings more than discreet classical works?   Yes ? No

202 Do you think it is futile to wonder about what there is in outer space?   Yes ? No

203 If you found something valuable in the street, would you pass it in to the police?   Yes ? No

204 Do you often feel bubbling over with excess energy?   Yes ? No

205 Do you often feel ill at ease with other people?   Yes ? No

206 Do you think that insurance schemes are a good idea?   Yes ? No

207 Do you get bored more easily than most people doing the same old things?   Yes ? No

208 Are you forever buying silly little gifts for people even though there is no occasion that calls for it?   Yes ? No

209 Do you spend much time reflecting upon the past and the shape that your life is taking?   Yes ? No

210 Would you describe yourself as 'happy go lucky'?   Yes ? No

The first personality factor which can be scored from the above questionnaire is called activity. People scoring high on this factor are generally active and energetic. They enjoy all kinds of physical activity including hard work and exercise. They tend to wake early and quickly in the morning, move rapidly from one activity to another, and pursue a wide variety of different interests. People with low scores on this scale are inclined to be physically inactive, lethargic and easily tired. They move about the world at a leisurely pace and prefer quiet, restful holidays. High activity is an extravert characteristic; low activity goes with introversion.

The key for scoring yourself on this scale is given below. The numbers refer to the item numbers in the questionnaire and the sign tells whether it is a 'Yes' or 'No' answer that should be given a point. As an example, consider Question 1: 'Are you happiest when you get involved in some project that calls for rapid action?' Because there is a plus sign after the number 1 in the key you give yourself a point if you answered with a 'Yes'. If you said 'No' you score nothing; if you responded with a '?' you score ½. Items 2-7 are not scored on this scale at all because they do not appear in the key. The next question that is scored on the activity scale is number 8, and again it is the 'Yes' which scores 1 because the sign is positive, while 'No' scores zero and '?' scores ½. The first question in the key to be reverse-scored is number 29: 'Are you inclined to be slow and deliberate in your actions?' This time, because the sign is a minus, it is the 'No' which scores 1 and the 'Yes' which scores zero; the '?' again scores ½.

To summarize then: only the question numbers that appear in the key are scored. If there is a plus sign the 'Yes' scores 1, if there is a minus sign the 'No' scores 1. In either case a '?' is scored ½. Each of the seven keys to follow includes thirty items, so the possible range of scores is 0 to 30. To see whether your scores are low, average or high in relation to other people, compare them with the profile sheet at the end of the chapter. This will also enable you to see whether you tend to be extraverted or introverted overall. Now here is the first key:

1 ACTIVITY

1	+	71	+	141	−
8	+	78	+	148	+
15	+	85	+	155	−
22	+	92	+	162	−
29	−	99	−	169	−
36	+	106	−	176	−
43	+	113	−	183	+
50	+	120	−	190	+
57	+	127	+	197	+
64	+	134	+	204	+

The second primary factor for which Questionnaire 1 may be scored is called sociability. This has a fairly straightforward interpretation. High scorers seek out the company of other people, they like social functions such as parties and dances, they meet people easily and are generally happy and comfortable in sociable situations. Low scorers, by contrast, prefer to have only a few special friends, enjoy solo activities such as reading, have difficulty finding things to talk about to other people, and are inclined to withdraw from oppressive social contacts. High sociability is an aspect of extraversion, low sociability goes with introversion. The key to this scale is given below and it is used in exactly the same way as the previous key.

2 SOCIABILITY

2	+	72	−	142	−
9	+	79	+	149	+
16	−	86	+	156	−
23	+	93	+	163	−
30	+	100	+	170	+
37	−	107	−	177	+
44	+	114	−	184	+
51	−	121	−	191	+
58	−	128	+	198	−
65	+	135	+	205	−

The third scale is called risk-taking and this is again fairly self-explanatory. High scorers like to live dangerously and seek rewards with little concern for the possible adverse consequences. Characteristically, they are gamblers who believe that 'an element of risk adds spice to life'. Low scores indicate a preference for familiarity, safety and security, even if this means sacrificing some degree of excitement in life. The risk-taking factor is quite closely related to 'impulsiveness', the next scale in the extraversion cluster. It is also quite closely related to 'sensation-seeking' which, it may surprise the reader to note, falls into the toughmindedness group of factors. This illustrates one of the complications of personality classification mentioned in the introduction, that a primary factor may fall diagonally between two major factors, just as the same item may contribute to two or more primary factors. The fact is that risk-taking and sensation-seeking may be used as measures of both extraversion and toughmindedness; they fall almost midway between the two independent major factors. However, because risk-taking is a little closer to the extraversion axis and sensation-seeking a little closer to the toughmindedness axis they have been classified accordingly. The key for risk-taking is given below:

3 RISK-TAKING

3	+	73	+	143	−
10	+	80	−	150	+
17	−	87	+	157	+
24	+	94	−	164	−
31	+	101	−	171	−
38	+	108	−	178	−
45	+	115	−	185	−
52	−	122	+	192	−
59	+	129	+	199	−
66	−	136	−	206	−

Scale 4 gives a measure of impulsiveness. High scorers are inclined to act on the spur of the moment, make hurried, often premature, decisions, and are usually carefree, changeable and unpredictable. Low scorers consider matters very carefully before making a decision. They are systematic, orderly, cautious, and plan their life out in advance; they think before they speak, and 'look before they leap'. The key for impulsiveness is given below:

4 IMPULSIVENESS

4	–	74	–	144	+
11	+	81	–	151	+
18	+	88	+	158	+
25	–	95	+	165	–
32	+	102	+	172	–
39	–	109	+	179	+
46	+	116	+	186	–
53	+	123	+	193	+
60	+	130	+	200	+
67	–	137	–	207	+

The fifth primary factory which goes to make up extraversion
has been labelled expressiveness. This refers to a general
tendency to display one's emotions outwardly and openly,
whether sorrow, anger, fear, love or hate. High scorers tend to
be sentimental, sympathetic, volatile and demonstrative; low
scorers are reserved, even-tempered, cool, detached, and
generally controlled as regards the expression of their thoughts
and feelings. This factor, taken to extreme, refers to behaviour
that is classically called 'hysterical', therefore it will come as no
surprise to learn that, even though it is primarily a component
of extraversion, it is also tilted slightly in the direction of
emotional instability.

5 EXPRESSIVENESS

5	−	75	+	145	+
12	+	82	+	152	+
19	+	89	−	159	−
26	+	96	+	166	+
33	−	103	+	173	−
40	+	110	+	180	−
47	−	117	−	187	+
54	+	124	−	194	+
61	−	131	−	201	+
68	+	138	−	208	+

The sixth component of extraversion is called reflectiveness. The slight complication with this scale is that high scores go towards the introversion end of the summary factor, and low scores go towards extraversion. In fact, some researchers in personality have called this factor 'thinking introversion', a useful label because it not only indicates the direction of the association with extraversion-introversion but it also distinguishes the trait from social introversion and emotional introversion (alternative though reverse-direction names for sociability and expressiveness). High scorers on our reflectiveness scale are inclined to be interested in ideas, abstractions, philosophical questions, discussions, speculations, and knowledge 'for the sake of knowledge'; that is, they are generally thoughtful (in the literal sense of the term) and introspective. Low scorers have a practical bent, are interested in doing things rather than thinking about them, and tend to be impatient with 'ivory tower' theorizing. Use the score key given below just as before and it will be clear from the profile sheet given at the end of the chapter whether your score is more indicative of extraversion or introversion.

6 REFLECTIVENESS

6	+	76	+	146	+
13	+	83	+	153	−
20	+	90	+	160	−
27	+	97	+	167	+
34	−	104	+	174	−
41	−	111	+	181	−
48	+	118	+	188	−
55	+	125	+	195	−
62	+	132	+	202	−
69	+	139	+	209	−

The last scale in this first batch is called responsibility, and this also goes with the introverted end of the spectrum rather than extraversion. People who score high on this factor are likely to be conscientious, reliable, trustworthy and serious-minded, possibly even a little bit compulsive (see obsessionality in the next cluster of traits). Low scorers, by contrast, are inclined to be casual, careless of protocol, late with commitments, unpredictable, and perhaps socially irresponsible. All this is within the normal range, however, so no implication of psychopathy or delinquency is intended even for rock-bottom scores. While it may be true to say that psychopaths and criminals are generally irresponsible, the converse is by no means certain; many people are low on this factor without having the slightest criminal inclination.

7 RESPONSIBILITY

7	+	77	−	147	+
14	+	84	−	154	−
21	+	91	+	161	−
28	+	98	−	168	−
35	−	105	+	175	+
42	−	112	−	182	+
49	−	119	+	189	−
56	−	126	−	196	−
63	−	133	+	203	+
70	−	140	+	210	−

By now you should have obtained seven scores, each falling in the range of 0 to 30. To see how you compare with the majority of other people you should mark your scores on the profile sheet given below, or on a tracing sheet if you do not want to mark the book. For example, if you scored 18 on Activity put a circle around the number 18 in the appropriate column, and so on for each of the other six primary traits. If you are above the central line you are higher than average on that trait; if you fall below you are below average (except of course for the two reverse-scored traits). It is necessary to think of the average in terms of a broad band, however, rather than exactly on the line. Also, it is important to remember that no evaluation, complimentary or condemnatory, is to be attached to extreme scores either high or low. Finally, if you connect up your seven scores with straight lines between each adjacent pair and look at the overall profile you will be able to see at a glance whether you are generally extraverted or introverted. If all or most of your scores fall above the centre line you are to a greater or lesser extent extraverted; if they fall consistently below the centre line you may regard yourself as an introvert.

EXTRAVERSION		AVERAGE		INTROVERSION

Extraversion trait	Extraversion scores	Average scores	Introversion trait
Activity	30 29 28 27 26 25 24 23 22 21 20 19 18 17	16 15 14 13 12 11 10 9 8 7 6 5 4 3 2 1	Inactivity
Sociability	30 29 28 27 26 25 24 23 22 21 20 19 18 17	16 15 14 13 12 11 10 9 8 7 6 5 4 3 2 1	Unsociability
Risk-taking	30 29 28 27 26 25 24 23 22 21 20 19 18 17 16	15 14 13 12 11 10 9 8 7 6 5 4 3 2 1 0	Carefulness
Impulsiveness	30 29 28 27 26 25 24 23 22 21 20 19 18	17 16 15 14 13 12 11 10 9 8 7 6 5 4 3 2	Control
Expressiveness	27 26 25 24 23 22 21 20 19 18 17 16 15 14 13 12	11 10 9 8 7 6 5 4 3 2	Inhibition
Practicality	2 3 4 5 6 7 8 9 10 11 12 13 14 15 16 17	18 19 20 21 22 23 24 25 26 27 28 29 30	Reflectiveness
Irresponsibility	0 1 2 3 4 5 6 7 8 9 10 11 12 13 14	15 16 17 18 19 20 21 22 23 24 25 26 27 28 29 30	Responsibility

3

EMOTIONAL INSTABILITY — ADJUSTMENT

The second major group of personality factors is concerned with the general area of emotional instability versus adjustment (sometimes called 'neuroticism' because people who are very emotionally unstable are more prone to neurotic illnesses). The 210 questions given below should be answered according to the same instructions as before; try to use the 'Yes' or 'No' if you possibly can and only resort to the '?' if you find it really impossible to decide. Again, do not worry unduly about the exact shade of meaning of each individual item; your first reaction is generally the best one.

Questionnaire

1 Do you think you are able to do things as well as most other people?   Yes   ?   No

2 Do you seem to have more than your share of bad luck?   Yes   ?   No

3 Do you blush more often than most people?   Yes   ?   No

4 Do you sometimes have ideas run through your head repeatedly that you would like to stop but can't?   Yes   ?   No

5 Is there some habit such as smoking that you would like to break but cannot?   Yes   ?   No

6 Do you usually feel well and strong?   Yes   ?   No

7 Are you often troubled by feelings of guilt?   Yes   ?   No

8   Do you feel that you have little to be proud of?   Yes   ?   No

9   Do you often feel depressed when you wake up in the mornings?   Yes   ?   No

10 Would you say that you seldom ever lose sleep over your worries?   Yes   ?   No

11 Are you often acutely aware of the ticking of clocks?   Yes   ?   No

12 If you see a game that you would like to be good at are you usually able to acquire the necessary skill to enjoy it?   Yes   ?   No

13 Do you often suffer from poor appetite?   Yes   ?   No

14 Do you often catch yourself apologising when you are not really at fault?   Yes   ?   No

15 Do you often think of yourself as a failure?   Yes   ?   No

16 In general would you say you are satisfied with your life?   Yes   ?   No

17 Are you usually calm and not easily upset?   Yes   ?   No

18 If you are reading something that contains errors of spelling and punctuation do you find it difficult to concentrate on what is being said?   Yes   ?   No

19 Do you take steps to control your figure by exercise or diet?   Yes   ?   No

20 Is your skin very sensitive and tender?   Yes   ?   No

21 Do you sometimes think you have let down your parents by the life you have led?   Yes   ?   No

22 Do you suffer from inferiority feelings?   Yes   ?   No

23 Do you find a good deal of happiness in life?   Yes   ?   No

24 Do you sometimes feel that you have so many difficulties that you cannot possibly overcome them?   Yes ? No

25 Are you sometimes compelled to wash your hands even though you know them to be perfectly clean?   Yes ? No

26 Do you believe that your personality was laid down firmly by the things that happened to you when you were a child, so that there isn't much you can do to change it?   Yes ? No

27 Do you frequently feel faint?   Yes ? No

28 Do you believe that you have committed unpardonable sins?   Yes ? No

29 In general are you pretty sure of yourself?   Yes ? No

30 Do you sometimes feel that you don't care what happens to you?   Yes ? No

31 Is life often a strain for you?   Yes ? No

32 Are you sometimes bothered by an unimportant thought that runs through your mind for days?   Yes ? No

33 Do you make your own decisions regardless of what other people say?   Yes ? No

34 Do you have more headaches than most people?   Yes ? No

35 Do you often feel a strong need to confess something that you have done?   Yes ? No

36 Do you often wish that you were someone else?   Yes ? No

37 Do you generally feel in good spirits?   Yes ? No

38 As a child were you afraid of the dark?   Yes ? No

39   Do you indulge in superstitious little
     rituals like avoiding the cracks in the pave-
     ment when you are walking along the foot-
     path?   Yes ? No

40   Do you find it difficult to control your
     weight?   Yes ? No

41   Do you sometimes feel a twitching of the
     face, head or shoulders?   Yes ? No

42   Do you often feel that people disapprove
     of you?   Yes ? No

43   Would you be troubled by feelings of
     inadequacy if you had to make a speech?   Yes ? No

44   Do you ever feel 'just miserable' for no
     good reason?   Yes ? No

45   Do you often feel restless as though you
     want something but do not really know
     what?   Yes ? No

46   Are you obsessional about locking up
     drawers, windows, suitcases and things?   Yes ? No

47   Do you place your trust in supernatural
     powers such as God or fate to see you
     through safely?   Yes ? No

48   Do you worry a lot about catching disease? Yes ? No

49   Do you believe that the pleasure you have
     in the here and now will have to be paid for
     eventually?   Yes ? No

50   Are there a lot of things about yourself
     that you would change if you could?   Yes ? No

51   Do you see your future as looking quite
     bright?   Yes ? No

52   Are you inclined to tremble and perspire if
     you are faced with a difficult task ahead? Yes ? No

53 Do you routinely check that all the lights, appliances and taps are off before you go to bed?   Yes ? No

54 If something goes wrong do you usually attribute it to bad luck rather than bad management?   Yes ? No

55 Do you make a point of visiting your doctor even if you think you only have a cold?   Yes ? No

56 Does it concern you a great deal that you are living better than the majority of people in the world?   Yes ? No

57 Do you think that you are quite popular with people in general?   Yes ? No

58 Have you ever wished you were dead?   Yes ? No

59 Are you often afraid of things and people that you know would not really hurt you?   Yes ? No

60 Are you careful to keep a supply of tinned or dried food in your house in case of an emergency food shortage?   Yes ? No

61 Have you ever felt as though you were possessed by evil spirits?   Yes ? No

62 Do you suffer a great deal from nervous exhaustion?   Yes ? No

63 Is there something you have done that you will regret all your life?   Yes ? No

64 Do you have a great deal of confidence in your decisions?   Yes ? No

65 Do you often feel down in the dumps?   Yes ? No

66 Are you less prone to anxiety than most of your friends?   Yes ? No

67 Does dirt frighten and disgust you to an exceptional degree?   Yes ? No

68 Do you often feel that you are a victim of
    outside forces that you cannot control?   Yes ? No

69 Are you considered a sickly person?   Yes ? No

70 Do you often get blamed or punished
    when you don't deserve it?   Yes ? No

71 Would you say that you have a high opin-
    ion of yourself?   Yes ? No

72 Do things often seem hopeless to you?   Yes ? No

73 Do you often worry unreasonably over
    things that do not really matter?   Yes ? No

74 If you are staying somewhere other than
    your own house do you make a point of
    planning how you would escape in the
    event of a fire?   Yes ? No

75 Do you set out to get what you want with a
    clear course of action rather than trusting
    to luck?   Yes ? No

76 Do you keep a medicine cabinet in your
    home that contains a great variety of left-
    overs from your previous prescriptions?   Yes ? No

77 Do you readily take it to heart if somebody
    scolds you?   Yes ? No

78 Do you often feel ashamed of things that
    you have done?   Yes ? No

79 Do you smile and laugh as much as most
    people?   Yes ? No

80 Are you anxious about something or some-
    body most of the time?   Yes ? No

81 Are you easily irritated by things that are
    out of place?   Yes ? No

82 Do you ever make decisions by tossing a
    coin or some such procedure that leaves it

entirely to chance? Yes ? No

83 Do you worry a great deal about your
health? Yes ? No

84 If you have an accident do you assume that
you must have deserved it because of
something you had done? Yes ? No

85 Do you feel embarrassed when looking at
photographs of yourself and complain
that they seldom do you justice? Yes ? No

86 Have you often felt listless and tired for no
good reason? Yes ? No

87 If you have made an awkward social error
can you forget it quite easily? Yes ? No

88 Do you keep very careful accounts of all
the money you spend? Yes ? No

89 Do you often act contrary to custom or to
the wishes of your parents? Yes ? No

90 Do severe pains and aches make it impossible for you to concentrate on your work? Yes ? No

91 Are you regretful about your early sexual
experiences? Yes ? No

92 Are there some members of your family
who make you feel you are not good
enough? Yes ? No

93 Are you often bothered by noise? Yes ? No

94 Can you relax quite easily when sitting or
lying down? Yes ? No

95 Do you worry a great deal about catching
germs from people in public? Yes ? No

96 If you were feeling lonely would you make
an effort to be friendly towards people? Yes ? No

97 Are you often bothered by severe itching? Yes ? No

98 Do you have some bad habits that are really inexcusable?   Yes ? No

99 Do you get very upset if someone criticises you?   Yes ? No

100 Do you feel that you often get a raw deal out of life?   Yes ? No

101 Are you easily startled by someone appearing unexpectedly?   Yes ? No

102 Are you always careful to pay back even the most trivial debt?   Yes ? No

103 Do you often feel that you have little influence over the things that happen to you? Yes ? No

104 Are you normally in good health?   Yes ? No

105 Are you often bothered by pangs of conscience?   Yes ? No

106 Do people regard you as useful to have around?   Yes ? No

107 Do you think that people really don't care what happens to you?   Yes ? No

108 Do you find it difficult to sit still without fidgeting?   Yes ? No

109 Do you often do jobs yourself rather than trust somebody else to do it properly?   Yes ? No

110 Are you easily persuaded by the arguments of other people?   Yes ? No

111 Does stomach trouble run in your family?   Yes ? No

112 Do you regard your youth as mis-spent?   Yes ? No

113 Are you often inclined to question your worth as a person?   Yes ? No

114 Do you often suffer from loneliness?   Yes ? No

115 Do you worry a great deal over money matters? Yes ? No

116 Would you walk under a ladder on the
street rather than go out of your way to
detour around it? Yes ? No

117 Do you often find life difficult to cope
with? Yes ? No

118 Are other people unsympathetic when you
are feeling unwell? Yes ? No

119 Do you think you are undeserving of other
people's trust and affection? Yes ? No

120 When people say nice things about you, do
you find it difficult to believe they are really
sincere? Yes ? No

121 Do you think you are contributing to the
world and leading a useful life? Yes ? No

122 Can you drop off to sleep quite easily at
night? Yes ? No

123 Can you easily disregard little mistakes
and inaccuracies? Yes ? No

124 Are most of the things you do geared to
pleasing other people? Yes ? No

125 Do you constantly suffer from constipa-
tion? Yes ? No

126 Do you spend a great deal of time going
over things that have happened in the past
and wishing that you had behaved more
responsibly? Yes ? No

127 Do you sometimes withhold your opinions
for fear that people will laugh and criticize
you? Yes ? No

128 Is there at least one person in the world
who really loves you? Yes ? No

129 Are you easily embarrassed in a social situation?   Yes ? No

130 Do you collect all kinds of scrap materials in case they might come in handy one day?   Yes ? No

131 Do you believe that your future is really in your own hands?   Yes ? No

132 Did you ever have a nervous breakdown?   Yes ? No

133 Are you harbouring a guilty secret that you are afraid must come out one day?   Yes ? No

134 Are you shy and self-conscious in social situations?   Yes ? No

135 Would you agree that it is hardly fair to bring a child into the world the way things look now?   Yes ? No

136 Are you easily 'rattled' if things don't go according to plan?   Yes ? No

137 Do you feel very uncomfortable if your home gets untidy?   Yes ? No

138 Have you as much will power as the next person?   Yes ? No

139 Are you often bothered by palpitations of the heart?   Yes ? No

140 Do you believe that bad behaviour will always be punished in the long run?   Yes ? No

141 Do you have a tendency to feel below the people you meet even though, objectively speaking, you are not outranked?   Yes ? No

142 Generally speaking have you been successful in achieving your aims and goals in life?   Yes ? No

143 Do you often wake up sweating after having a bad dream?   Yes ? No

144 Are you repelled if somebody's pet dog
licks you on the face?　　　　　　Yes ? No

145 Do you find it a waste of time planning
ahead because something always turns up
that causes you to change your plans?　Yes ? No

146 Do you worry a lot about other members of
your family getting ill?　　　　　　Yes ? No

147 If you have done something morally reprehensible can you quickly forget it and
direct your thoughts to the future?　Yes ? No

148 Do you usually feel that you can accom-
plish the things you want to?　　　Yes ? No

149 Are you often overcome by sadness?　Yes ? No

150 Does your voice get shaky if you are talking
to someone you particularly want to impress?　Yes ? No

151 Would you rather go without something
than feel obliged to another person?　Yes ? No

152 Would you prefer a job in which somebody else made the decisions and told you
what to do?　　　　　　　　　Yes ? No

153 Are you troubled by cold hands and feet
even in warm weather?　　　　　Yes ? No

154 Do you often pray for forgiveness?　Yes ? No

155 Are you satisfied with your appearance?　Yes ? No

156 Does it seem to you that it is always other
people who get the breaks?　　　Yes ? No

157 Would you stay calm and collected in the
face of an emergency?　　　　　Yes ? No

158 Do you make a point of writing down all
your appointments in a note book, even
things you have to do later in the same
day?　　　　　　　　　　　Yes ? No

159 Do you often get the feeling that it's no use
    trying to get anywhere in life?   Yes ? No

160 Do you often have difficulty in breathing?   Yes ? No

161 Are you embarrassed by dirty stories?   Yes ? No

162 Are you often reticent with other people
    because you think they will not like you?   Yes ? No

163 Is it a long time since you last felt on top of
    the world?   Yes ? No

164 Do you sometimes get into a state of ten-
    sion and turmoil when thinking over your
    difficulties?   Yes ? No

165 Do you usually adjust your hair and cloth-
    ing before you open the door to a visitor?   Yes ? No

166 Do you often feel that you don't have
    enough control over the direction that
    your life is taking?   Yes ? No

167 Do you think it is a waste of time going to
    the doctor with most mild complaints such
    as coughs, colds and influenza?   Yes ? No

168 Do you often feel as though you have done
    something wrong and wicked even though
    this feeling is not really justified?   Yes ? No

169 Do you find it difficult to do things in a
    way that wins the attention and approval
    of others?   Yes ? No

170 Do you feel cheated when you look back on
    what has happened to you?   Yes ? No

171 Do you worry too long over humiliating
    experiences?   Yes ? No

172 Are you often tempted to correct people's
    grammar when you are talking to them
    (although politeness may prevent you
    from doing so)?   Yes ? No

173 Do you find that things are changing so fast today that it is difficult to know what rules to follow?   Yes   ?   No

174 Do you always go straight to bed if you have caught a cold?   Yes   ?   No

175 Do you think that you must have disappointed your teachers at school by not working hard enough?   Yes   ?   No

176 Do you often catch yourself pretending to be a better person than you really are?   Yes   ?   No

177 Are you about as happy as the next person?   Yes   ?   No

178 Would you describe yourself as self-conscious?   Yes   ?   No

179 Would you describe yourself as a perfectionist?   Yes   ?   No

180 Do you usually have clear-cut goals and a sense of purpose in life?   Yes   ?   No

181 Do you look at the colour of your tongue most mornings?   Yes   ?   No

182 Do you often think back on how badly you have treated people in the past?   Yes   ?   No

183 Do you sometimes feel that you can never do anything right?   Yes   ?   No

184 Do you often get the feeling that you are just not a part of things?   Yes   ?   No

185 Do you worry unnecessarily over things that might happen?   Yes   ?   No

186 Do you go through a set routine on retiring to bed that if broken would cause you great difficulty in getting to sleep?   Yes   ?   No

187 Do you often have the feeling that other
people are using you?   Yes   ?   No

188 Do you weigh yourself every day?   Yes   ?   No

189 Do you expect God will punish you for
your sins in the after-life?   Yes   ?   No

190 Do you often have doubts about your sex-
ual prowess?   Yes   ?   No

191 Is your sleep usually fitful and disturbed?   Yes   ?   No

192 Are you inclined to get yourself all worked
up over nothing?   Yes   ?   No

193 Is it very important to you that everything
should always be neat and tidy?   Yes   ?   No

194 Are you sometimes influenced by advertise-
ments to buy something you didn't really
want?   Yes   ?   No

195 Are you often troubled by noises in your
ears?   Yes   ?   No

196 Do you usually blame yourself if something goes wrong with your personal rela-
tionships?   Yes   ?   No

197 Have you at least a normal amount of self
respect?   Yes   ?   No

198 Do you often feel lonely even when you are
with other people?   Yes   ?   No

199 Have you ever felt you needed to take tranquillizers?   Yes   ?   No

200 Are you very upset if your daily habits are
disturbed by unforeseen events?   Yes   ?   No

201 Do you read horoscopes with the hope of
obtaining some guidance in your life?   Yes   ?   No

202 Do you often feel a choking lump in your
    throat?   Yes ? No

203 Are you sometimes disgusted by your own
    sexual desires and fantasies?   Yes ? No

204 Do you think your personality is attractive
    to the opposite sex?   Yes ? No

205 Do you feel a sense of inner calm and con-
    tentment most of the time?   Yes ? No

206 Are you a nervous person?   Yes ? No

207 Do you spend a great deal of time filing
    and arranging your papers so you will be
    certain to know where everything is if
    you should want it?   Yes ? No

208 Do other people usually decide what play
    or film you are going to see?   Yes ? No

209 Do you have hot or cold spells?   Yes ? No

210 Is it easy for you to forget the things that
    you have done wrong?   Yes ? No

The first scale that can be derived from the above questionnaire is called self-esteem. People who score high on self-esteem tend to have plenty of confidence in themselves and their abilities. They think of themselves as worthy, useful human beings, and believe that they are well-liked by other people. Without necessarily implying cockiness or conceit it could be said that they like themselves a lot. Low scorers have a low opinion of themselves, believing that they are unattractive failures. An extreme low score may be thought of as approximating to the celebrated 'inferiority complex' which was such a fashionable concept with American psychiatrists a decade or so ago.

The key for this scale is given below. It is used in the same way as those given in Chapter 2: when the sign is plus, score 1 for a 'Yes'; when the sign is minus score 1 for a 'No'. The '?' scores ½ regardless of the sign. Remember only to score for the question numbers listed in the key.

1 SELF-ESTEEM

1	+	71	+	141	−
8	−	78	−	148	+
15	−	85	−	155	+
22	−	92	−	162	−
29	+	99	−	169	−
36	−	106	+	176	−
43	−	113	−	183	−
50	−	120	−	190	−
57	+	127	−	197	+
64	+	134	−	204	+

The second scale we have called happiness, and the meaning of this is very straightforward. High scorers are generally cheerful, optimistic and well. They are satisfied with their existence, find life rewarding, and are at peace with the world. Low scorers are characteristically pessimistic, gloomy and depressed, disappointed with their existence and at odds with the world.

The key for this scale is given below. At what point should the reader consider himself as clinically depressed? There is no particular cut-off point that can be meaningfully used in this way. Our scale was constructed to cover the normal range of happiness-unhappiness; nevertheless, it is possible that an extreme low scorer does have a depressive illness. If the reader thinks this could be the case he or she might consider consulting a doctor. Some kinds of depression respond to special drugs; other kinds may be helped with behavioural psychotherapy.

2 HAPPINESS

2	−	72	−	142	+
9	−	79	+	149	−
16	+	86	−	156	−
23	+	93	−	163	−
30	−	100	−	170	−
37	+	107	−	177	+
44	−	114	−	184	−
51	+	121	+	191	−
58	−	128	+	198	−
65	−	135	−	205	+

Scale 3 is labelled anxiety. High scorers are easily upset by things that go wrong and are inclined to worry unnecessarily about things that may or may not happen. Such people account for a high proportion of the consumption of minor tranquillizers like Librium and Valium. Low scorers are placid, serene and resistant to irrational fears and anxieties. On average, women admit to a higher degree of fear and anxiety than men, but the difference is not so outstanding as to necessitate separate keys for the two sexes.

3 ANXIETY

3	+	73	+	143	+
10	−	80	+	150	+
17	−	87	−	157	−
24	+	94	−	164	+
31	+	101	+	171	+
38	+	108	+	178	+
45	+	115	+	185	+
52	+	122	−	192	+
59	+	129	+	199	+
66	−	136	+	206	+

The fourth type of 'maladjustment' represented in our questionnaire is obsessiveness. High scorers are careful, conscientious, highly disciplined, staid, finicky, and easily irritated by things that are unclean, untidy or out of place. Low scorers are casual and easy-going, with less need for order, routine or ritual. Again, the questions are selected to cover a normal range, so the scale cannot really be used to diagnose an obsessive-compulsive neurosis in the sense that a psychiatrist would understand. But if a person's life is so dominated by unwelcome, repetitive thoughts or habits that they are completely incapacitated, they should certainly see a doctor because effective treatments are now available.

4 OBSESSIVENESS

4	+	74	+	144	+
11	+	81	+	151	+
18	+	88	+	158	+
25	+	95	+	165	+
32	+	102	+	172	+
39	+	109	+	179	+
46	+	116	−	186	+
53	+	123	−	193	+
60	+	130	+	200	+
67	+	137	+	207	+

The fifth scale is called autonomy. The autonomous person (high scorer) enjoys a great deal of freedom and independence, makes his own decisions, views himself as the master of his own fate and takes realistic action to solve his problems. The low scorer lacks self-reliance, thinks of himself as a helpless pawn of fate, is pushed around by other people and events, and shows a high degree of what has been called 'authoritarian submission' —the unquestioning obedience to institutional power. Men tend to score very slightly higher on this scale, but again not so strikingly that separate norms need be provided.

5 AUTONOMY

5	−	75	+	145	−
12	+	82	−	152	−
19	+	89	+	159	−
26	−	96	+	166	−
33	+	103	−	173	−
40	−	110	−	180	+
47	−	117	−	187	−
54	−	124	−	194	−
61	−	131	+	201	−
68	−	138	+	208	−

The sixth scale, hypochondriasis, measures a tendency to acquire psychosomatic symptoms and imagine that one is ill. High scorers complain of a wide variety of diffuse physical symptoms, show a great deal of concern about their state of health, and frequently demand the sympathetic attention of their doctor and their family and friends. Low scorers are very seldom ill and do not worry very much about their health. It is just possible that a high score on this scale could be obtained by an individual who is genuinely very sick physically, but the variety of symptoms sampled makes this extremely unlikely.

6 HYPOCHONDRIASIS

6	−	76	+	146	+
13	+	83	+	153	+
20	+	90	+	160	+
27	+	97	+	167	−
34	+	104	−	174	+
41	+	111	+	181	+
48	+	118	+	188	+
55	+	125	+	195	+
62	+	132	+	202	+
69	+	139	+	209	+

Finally, we have included a scale for guilt. High scorers are self-blaming, self-abasing and troubled by their conscience regardless of whether or not their behaviour is really morally reprehensible. Low scorers are little inclined to punish themselves or regret their past behaviour. A certain level of guilt may be appropriate for some people (indeed its complete absence is symptomatic of psychopathy) but excessive self-recrimination is usually regarded as a neurotic characteristic. Extreme high scorers often have a strict religious background but this is by no means a complete and adequate explanation.

7 GUILT

7	+	77	+	147	−
14	+	84	+	154	+
21	+	91	+	161	+
28	+	98	+	168	+
35	+	105	+	175	+
42	+	112	+	182	+
49	+	119	+	189	+
56	+	126	+	196	+
63	+	133	+	203	+
70	−	140	+	210	−

Having obtained seven scores from the questionnaire, these can be entered onto the profile sheet below (as for Chapter 2). Then, one's overall emotional instability or adjustment can be assessed at a glance. If the scores fall consistently and clearly above the centre line, a certain degree of instability is indicated. If the scores fall around the centre line or below, the reader can regard himself or herself as reasonably stable or 'well balanced'.

Whereas we said that no evaluation, good or bad, could be applied to positions along the extraversion-introversion axis, this is clearly not quite the case here. Most people would agree that it is better to be stable in that extreme emotionality usually carries a great deal of suffering and unhappiness. On the other hand, some people would argue that excessive stability is also undesirable because to live is to experience, and the person who feels nothing may as well be dead. Remember also that, as pointed out in the introduction, very emotional people often have the advantage when it comes to artistic pursuits. Perhaps the middle (normal) area is optimal. This is a complex debate and we do not propose to take sides or pursue it here.

	EMOTIONAL INSTABILITY		AVERAGE		STABILITY ADJUSTMENT
Inferiority feelings	6 7 8 9 10 11 12 13 14 15 16 17 18 19 20 21		22	23 24 25 26 27 28 29 30	Self-esteem
Depressiveness	7 8 9 10 11 12 13 14 15 16 17 18 19 20 21 22		23	24 25 26 27 28 29 30	Happiness
Anxiety	30 29 28 27 26 25 24 23 22 21 20 19 18 17 16		15	14 13 12 11 10 9 8 7 6 5	Calm
Obsessiveness	25 24 23 22 21 20 19 18 17 16 15 14 13 13 11 10		9	8 7 6 5 4 3 2 1	Casualness
Dependence	5 6 7 8 9 10 11 12 13 14 15 16 17 18 19 20		21	22 23 24 25 26 27 28 29	Autonomy
Hypochondriasis	21 20 19 18 17 16 15 14 13 12 11 10 9 8 7 6		5	4 3 2 1	Sense of health
Guilt	23 22 21 20 19 18 17 16 15 14 13 12 11 10 9 8		7	6 5 4 3 2 1 0	Guilt-freedom

4 | TOUGHMINDEDNESS - TENDERMINDEDNESS

The third group of personality factors is probably best summarized by the label 'toughmindedness versus tendermindedness'. The questionnaire dealing with behaviours in this area is given below. As before, work through it quickly giving 'Yes' or 'No' answers whenever possible and only using '?' if absolutely necessary.

Questionnaire

1	If someone does you a bad turn do you feel obliged to do something about it?	Yes	?	No
2	Would you rebuke a friend if you disapproved of his behaviour?	Yes	?	No
3	Do you have a strong desire to be an important person in the community?	Yes	?	No
4	Do you prefer to conceal from other people what your motives are for doing things?	Yes	?	No
5	Do you like a great deal of variety and change in your life?	Yes	?	No
6	Do you find it difficult to stop once you get wound up into a heated discussion?	Yes	?	No
7	Do you like to engage in rough physical activity?	Yes	?	No
8	Would you like to watch an execution if you were given the opportunity?	Yes	?	No

9   Do you try to get your own way regardless
    of opposition?   Yes   ?   No

10 Do you set your aspirations low in order to
    avoid disappointments?   Yes   ?   No

11 Would you be more upset by losing some
    valuable property than hearing that a
    friend was seriously ill?   Yes   ?   No

12 Would you like to ride in a racing car at
    150 miles per hour?   Yes   ?   No

13 Do you think it is dangerous to compro-
    mise with political opponents?   Yes   ?   No

14 At school, did you prefer English litera-
    ture over general science?   Yes   ?   No

15 Do you think that if someone is rude to you
    it is best to let it pass?   Yes   ?   No

16 If someone went to the front of a queue out
    of turn would you do something about it?   Yes   ?   No

17 Would you describe yourself as an ambi-
    tious person?   Yes   ?   No

18 Do you think that honesty is always the
    best policy?   Yes   ?   No

19 Do you like to be in a climate that has very
    even temperatures?   Yes   ?   No

20 Would you prefer to be a dead hero than a
    live coward?   Yes   ?   No

21 Do you enjoy reading romantic stories?   Yes   ?   No

22 Have you ever felt as though you would
    genuinely like to kill somebody?   Yes   ?   No

23 If somebody smoking nearby was annoy-
    ing you would you ask them to stop?   Yes   ?   No

24 Do you work hard for success rather than
    daydream about it?   Yes   ?   No

25 Do you think that politicians are generally
sincere and doing their best for the
country?   Yes ? No

26 Would mountain climbing be too dangerous for you to consider as a sport for your-
self?   Yes ? No

27 Are you forthright and uncompromising
in argument?   Yes ? No

28 Are you very sensitive to beauty in your
surroundings?   Yes ? No

29 Do you get very angry when you read what
certain politicians have said in the news-
paper?   Yes ? No

30 Do you believe that it is necessary to fight
for your rights otherwise you risk losing
them altogether?   Yes ? No

31 Do you have any tendency towards lazi-
ness?   Yes ? No

32 Do you sometimes tell people what they
want to hear so that they will be more
receptive to you?   Yes ? No

33 Would you take drugs that were likely to
have strange effects on you such as causing
hallucinations?   Yes ? No

34 Do you believe that the 'tried and true'
ways are always the best?   Yes ? No

35 Do you enjoy shopping?   Yes ? No

36 Do you like to watch boxing or wrestling
matches on television?   Yes ? No

37 Do you express your opinions very force-
fully?   Yes ? No

38 Do you try to do things immediately rather
than put them off until later?   Yes ? No

39 Do you think that fools deserve to be par-
    ted from their money?   Yes   ?   No

40 Does the sport of scuba-diving appeal to
    you?   Yes   ?   No

41 Do you have very clear ideas about what is
    right and wrong?   Yes   ?   No

42 Do you feel like crying if you see a sad film? Yes   ?   No

43 Do you ever get so angry with other people
    that you yell and swear at them?   Yes   ?   No

44 Do you make a point of complaining if you
    are sold shoddy goods?   Yes   ?   No

45 Do you pursue your work with relentless
    determination?   Yes   ?   No

46 Are you adept in the use of white lies?   Yes   ?   No

47 Do you prefer to avoid the more 'hair
    raising' rides at amusement parks?   Yes   ?   No

48 Once you have made up your mind about
    something do you stick to your decision
    come what may?   Yes   ?   No

49 Are you afraid of creepy-crawly things
    such as worms and spiders?   Yes   ?   No

50 Do you quickly forgive people who let you
    down?   Yes   ?   No

51 Do you hold your views less strongly than
    other people?   Yes   ?   No

52 If you had to sit an examination during
    your school years did you do a great deal
    of preparation for it?   Yes   ?   No

53 Do you agree that it is naive and danger-
    ous to place your complete trust in another
    person?   Yes   ?   No

54 Do you like to mix with people who are
    wild and unpredictable?   Yes ? No

55 Do you believe there is only one true reli-
    gion?   Yes ? No

56 Do the laws of physics interest you more
    than personal relationships?   Yes ? No

57 Did you stay out of physical fights when
    you were a child?   Yes ? No

58 Are you intimidated by people in authori-
    ty?   Yes ? No

59 Do days sometimes go by without your
    having done a thing?   Yes ? No

60 Do you sometimes use flattery consciously
    to assist in gaining your own ends?   Yes ? No

61 Would you like to learn to fly an aero-
    plane?   Yes ? No

62 Do you often question your own morality
    and rules of conduct?   Yes ? No

63 Do you sometimes have sadistic fantasies? Yes ? No

64 Do you think that most pacifists are just
    cowards?   Yes ? No

65 As a child did you usually do as you were
    told?   Yes ? No

66 Do you find it difficult to enjoy a holiday
    because you would prefer to be back at
    work?   Yes ? No

67 Do you believe it is necessary to cut corners
    here and there in order to get on in the
    world?   Yes ? No

68 In general, do you dislike hot, spicy and
    exotic dishes?   Yes ? No

69 Do you agree that most politicians talk a
    load of rubbish?   Yes ? No

70 Do you like going to dances?   Yes ? No

71 Do you often grind your teeth consciously
    or unconsciously?   Yes ? No

72 If somebody in a theatre was wearing a hat
    that obscured your view would you rather
    find another seat than ask them to remove
    it?   Yes ? No

73 Do you often compare your ability and
    performance on a job with that of other
    people?   Yes ? No

74 Are you generally cool and detached in
    your dealings with other people?   Yes ? No

75 Would you consider going to a wife-
    swapping party?   Yes ? No

76 Do you think people with extreme political
    views should be allowed to air them in
    public?   Yes ? No

77 Do you like scenes of violence and torture
    in the movies?   Yes ? No

78 Would you say that you lose your temper
    less often than most people?   Yes ? No

79 Do you usually make the decisions when
    you are with a group of people?   Yes ? No

80 Are you sometimes so excited by your work
    that thinking about it keeps you awake at
    night?   Yes ? No

81 Does a sense of fair play restrict your busi-
    ness acumen?   Yes ? No

82 Do you prefer paintings that are quiet and
    discreet rather than vivid and shocking to
    the sense?   Yes ? No

83 In the case of a disagreement do you try to put yourself in the other person's position and try to understand his point of view? Yes ? No

84 Would the sight of a great deal of blood make you feel faint? Yes ? No

85 Do you sometimes get so annoyed that you break crockery or throw things around the house? Yes ? No

86 If you have been given poor service in a restaurant or hotel do you prefer to let it pass rather than make a fuss? Yes ? No

87 Are you inclined to be very envious of the success of other people? Yes ? No

88 If you want someone to do something for you do you tell them your true reasons rather than offer reasons which might be more acceptable and persuasive? Yes ? No

89 Are you unusually susceptible to boredom? Yes ? No

90 Do you attempt to convert others to your own point of view on matters of religion, morality and politics? Yes ? No

91 Are you 'turned off' by crude and vulgar jokes? Yes ? No

92 Do you like to play at ducking people when you are having a swim? Yes ? No

93 Do you prefer to stay in the background rather than push yourself forward? Yes ? No

94 Do you get excited when you are telling someone else about the work you do? Yes ? No

95 Do you feel a great deal of sympathy for the underdog? Yes ? No

96 Do you sometimes say something shocking just to see how people will react to it? Yes ? No

97 Do you sometimes argue for the sake of
    argument, even when you know under-
    neath that you are wrong?   Yes ? No

98 Do you rely on intuition as a guide to
    whether or not a person is trustworthy?   Yes ? No

99 Do you often blame other people when
    something goes wrong?   Yes ? No

100 Do you agree with the philosophy of 'every
    man for himself'?   Yes ? No

101 Is it extremely important to you to 'get on
    in the world'?   Yes ? No

102 Are you drawn toward people who are sick
    and unfortunate?   Yes ? No

103 Do you enjoy horror movies such as
    Dracula and Frankenstein?   Yes ? No

104 Do you find that your own way of attack-
    ing a problem always turns out to be the
    best in the long run?   Yes ? No

105 Do you occasionally break down and cry?   Yes ? No

106 Are you usually able to refrain from ex-
    pressing your irritation?   Yes ? No

107 Do you usually dissociate yourself from
    political protests?   Yes ? No

108 Do you enjoy reading about the lives of
    famous people?   Yes ? No

109 Do you think that most people are basic-
    ally good and kind?   Yes ? No

110 If you were offered an opportunity to go
    around the moon in a space-ship would
    you accept?   Yes ? No

111 Does it annoy you when a supposed expert
    fails to come up with a definite solution to

a social problem? Yes ? No

112 Do you enjoy watching competitive physical sports such as boxing and football? Yes ? No

113 If somebody annoys you do you usually tell him what you think of him in no uncertain terms? Yes ? No

114 Do you think that playing the game in a sporting manner is more important than winning a contest? Yes ? No

115 Do you try to enjoy your work from day to day rather than striving to improve your position? Yes ? No

116 Do you occasionally have to hurt other people to get what you want? Yes ? No

117 Would you rather mix with people of your own kind than with foreigners who have customs that are strange to you? Yes ? No

118 Do you think it would be a good thing if everybody shared the same ideas and values? Yes ? No

119 Are you somewhat frightened of the dark? Yes ? No

120 Would you rather say you agree with somebody than start an argument? Yes ? No

121 Do you always argue a point if you think you are right? Yes ? No

122 Do you find it difficult to concentrate on what people are saying to you when you are working on an important job? Yes ? No

123 Do you usually take care of your own interests before worrying about those of other people? Yes ? No

124 Would you enjoy seeing a pornographic

film?   Yes   ?   No

125 Are you inclined to see things in various
    shades of grey rather than in black and
    white?   Yes   ?   No

126 Are you very interested in science fiction?   Yes   ?   No

127 When you get into a rage do you do a lot
    of physical things like stamping your feet
    and kicking things?   Yes   ?   No

128 Do you hesitate to ask a stranger for a
    street direction?   Yes   ?   No

129 Can you easily forget about your work
    when you are on holiday?   Yes   ?   No

130 Do some of your friends regard you as too
    good-natured and easily taken in?   Yes   ?   No

131 Do you sometimes do slightly dangerous
    things 'just for the hell of it'?   Yes   ?   No

132 Do you think a good teacher is one who
    makes you wonder rather than telling you
    all the answers?   Yes   ?   No

133 Do you find it difficult to resist picking up
    and cuddling small furry animals?   Yes   ?   No

134 Can you usually manage to be patient,
    even with fools?   Yes   ?   No

135 Are you too often 'pushed around' by
    other people?   Yes   ?   No

136 Are you satisfied with the amount of
    money you are getting at the moment?   Yes   ?   No

137 Do you normally tell the truth even though
    you might be better off lying?   Yes   ?   No

138 Would you avoid seeing a disaster movie in
    which thousands of people and an entire
    city were destroyed by earthquake and fire? Yes   ?   No

139 Does your blood boil when people stubbornly refuse to admit they are wrong?   Yes ? No

140 Do you often think about falling in love?   Yes ? No

141 Do you often make biting or sarcastic remarks about other people?   Yes ? No

142 Would you rather take orders than give them?   Yes ? No

143 Would you very much enjoy being 'in the public eye'?   Yes ? No

144 Are you generally able to persuade other people to do what you want them to?   Yes ? No

145 Would you like to try parachute jumping?   Yes ? No

146 Are you often uncertain as to which way you are going to vote in an election?   Yes ? No

147 Do you startle easily if somebody surprises you with a sudden appearance?   Yes ? No

148 Are there times when you feel as though you would like to pick a fight with somebody?   Yes ? No

149 Do you always stand up for your rights?   Yes ? No

150 Have you ever tried to model your career on that of a successful person?   Yes ? No

151 Would you put yourself out a great deal to help somebody who was suffering an emotional hurt?   Yes ? No

152 Do you prefer Mozart to Wagner?   Yes ? No

153 Do you think that other cultures have a lot to teach us about how to live?   Yes ? No

154 Would you consider taking part in an orgy?   Yes ? No

155 Is the shooting gallery one of your

favourite attractions at a fun fair?   Yes ? No

156 Do you always obey 'no trespassing' and
    'keep off the grass' signs?   Yes ? No

157 If you catch yourself being lazy do you try
    to do something about it immediately?   Yes ? No

158 Do you tend to get very closely involved
    with other people so that you share their
    troubles and give them emotional
    support?   Yes ? No

159 Do you dislike people who play practical
    jokes all the time?   Yes ? No

160 Do you find it easy to be friendly with
    people of different religions from your
    own?   Yes ? No

161 Would you enjoy singing in a church
    choir?   Yes ? No

162 Are you considered an even-tempered
    person?   Yes ? No

163 Would you like to appear on television
    stating your political opinions?   Yes ? No

164 Do you take an unusual amount of pride in
    your work?   Yes ? No

165 Do you gain a lot of pleasure out of helping
    other people?   Yes ? No

166 Do you like plenty of bustle and excite-
    ment going on around you?   Yes ? No

167 Do you think it is often necessary to use
    force to advance an idea?   Yes ? No

168 Are you curious about the workings of
    engines and other mechanical devices?   Yes ? No

169 Would you hesitate to shoot a burglar who
    was escaping with some of your property?   Yes ? No

170 Do you hesitate to take a front seat in a lecture room because you don't like to be conspicuous?　　　　Yes ? No

171 Do you have a strong desire to 'better yourself'?　　　　Yes ? No

172 Do you think that there are better reasons for getting married than being in love?　　　　Yes ? No

173 Would you find it very difficult to leave your home and friends and travel to a new part of the world to live?　　　　Yes ? No

174 Do you change your mind readily if someone puts up a convincing argument?　　　　Yes ? No

175 Do you like war stories?　　　　Yes ? No

176 If you meet a person who is conceited and domineering are you inclined to put him in his place?　　　　Yes ? No

177 Are you good at bluffing your way out of difficult situations?　　　　Yes ? No

178 Do you prefer to mix with people who can help you make your way in the world?　　　　Yes ? No

179 Would you befriend someone you did not really like if you thought he might be a useful contact?　　　　Yes ? No

180 Would you enjoy a life of peace and serenity?　　　　Yes ? No

181 Do you think there is a kernel of truth in nearly everybody's point of view?　　　　Yes ? No

182 Would you enjoy painting pictures of children?　　　　Yes ? No

183 Do you enjoy scenes of gladiators fighting in the movies?　　　　Yes ? No

184 Do you find it difficult to get rid of a sales-

man who is persistent and wasting your
time?   Yes   ?   No

185 Do you strive very hard to get ahead?   Yes   ?   No

186 Can you easily disregard the feelings of
other people in order to deal more expedi-
ently with them?   Yes   ?   No

187 Do you often long for excitement?   Yes   ?   No

188 Do you often repeat yourself to make sure
that you are properly understood?   Yes   ?   No

189 Do you feel deeply sorry for a bird with a
broken wing?   Yes   ?   No

190 In general are you satisfied with the way
the country is being run?   Yes   ?   No

191 Can you always think of a good excuse if
the situation demands it?   Yes   ?   No

192 Do you let an escalator carry you along
without walking yourself?   Yes   ?   No

193 Do you often plan what you are going to
say before you meet someone?   Yes   ?   No

194 Is boredom one of the things you fear most
of all?   Yes   ?   No

195 Do you carefully consider everybody else's
viewpoint before arriving at your own?   Yes   ?   No

196 Would you rather be a dentist than a
dress-designer?   Yes   ?   No

197 Are you often extremely furious with other
people even though you restrain yourself
from letting them know?   Yes   ?   No

198 Do you sometimes wish you could be more
assertive?   Yes   ?   No

199 Is achievement one of your primary
values?   Yes   ?   No

200 Is love more important to you than
success?   Yes ? No

201 Would you like to hunt lions in darkest
Africa?   Yes ? No

202 Do you determine nearly all of your con-
duct in relation to a single great cause?   Yes ? No

203 Are snakes abhorrent to you?   Yes ? No

204 Do you like debates to be hard-hitting with
no punches held and no holds barred?   Yes ? No

205 If you were working on a committee would
you tend to take charge of things?   Yes ? No

206 Do you devote a great deal of energy toward making a creative contribution to
society?   Yes ? No

207 Do you regard yourself as a skilled organi-
zer and manipulator of other people?   Yes ? No

208 Can you enjoy sex sufficiently without
having to resort to perversions?   Yes ? No

209 Are you appalled by the ignorance shown
by the majority of people on social and
political matters?   Yes ? No

210 As a child did you enjoy playing with guns?   Yes ? No

Our first scale in the toughmindedness cluster of traits is that of aggressiveness. High scorers are given to the direct or indirect expression of aggression, for example through behaviours such as temper tantrums, fighting, violent argument and sarcasm. They take no nonsense from anyone and feel compelled to re-turn fire or 'get back' at anyone who transgresses against them. Low scorers are gentle, even-tempered, prefer to avoid personal conflict, and are not given to violence either physical or indirect. As with all the scales in this cluster, males score higher on average, and since the difference is real in the sense that it almost certainly is biologically based, it would be misleading to make a sex correction in the norms. The key for aggressiveness is given below; use it in the manner described in Chapter 2.

1 AGGRESSIVENESS

1	+	71	+	141	+
8	+	78	−	148	+
15	−	85	+	155	+
22	+	92	+	162	−
29	+	99	+	169	−
36	+	106	−	176	+
43	+	113	+	183	+
50	−	120	−	190	−
57	−	127	+	197	+
64	+	134	−	204	+

The second scale is called assertiveness. This is closely related to aggressiveness but is a slightly more civilized form. High scorers have what is sometimes called a 'strong personality'; they are independent, dominant, and stand up for their rights, perhaps to the extent of being viewed as 'pushy'. Low scorers are humble, timid, submissive, disinclined to take any initiative in an interpersonal situation, and may be easily imposed upon.

2 ASSERTIVENESS

2	+	72	−	142	−
9	+	79	+	149	+
16	+	86	−	156	−
23	+	93	−	163	+
30	+	100	+	170	−
37	+	107	−	177	+
44	+	114	−	184	−
51	−	121	+	191	+
58	−	128	−	198	−
65	−	135	−	205	+

The third scale is called achievement orientation. High scorers are ambitious, hard-working, competitive, keen to improve their social standing, and place a high value on productivity and creativity. Low scorers place little value on competitive performance or creative output. Many are also apathetic, retiring and aimless, but these are not invariable characteristics of the person without strong achievement motivation.

3 ACHIEVEMENT ORIENTATION

3	+	73	+	143	+
10	−	80	+	150	+
17	+	87	+	157	+
24	+	94	+	164	+
31	−	101	+	171	+
38	+	108	+	178	+
45	+	115	−	185	+
52	+	122	+	192	−
59	−	129	−	199	+
66	+	136	−	206	+

The fourth scale is called manipulation. High scorers are detached, calculating, shrewd, worldly, expedient, and self-interested in their dealings with other people. Low scorers are warm-hearted, trusting, empathetic, straightforward and altruistic, perhaps also a little naive and gullible. This trait is sometimes called Machiavellianism because it corresponds to some extent with the political philosophy expounded by the Italian writer Niccolo Machiavelli (a sort of renaissance Henry Kissinger).

4 MANIPULATION

4	+	74	+	144	+
11	+	81	−	151	−
18	−	88	−	158	−
25	−	95	−	165	−
32	+	102	−	172	+
39	+	109	−	179	+
46	+	116	+	186	+
53	+	123	+	193	+
60	+	130	−	200	−
67	+	137	−	207	+

Scale 5 is called sensation-seeking, and this title is fairly self-explanatory. High scorers are forever seeking thrills in life; they have an insatiable thirst for novel experiences and require regular 'jags' in order to stave off boredom. To this end they will accept a moderate level of danger to life and limb. Low scorers have little need for excitement or adventure; instead they prefer the secure and familiar comforts of 'home'. The association of this dare-devil 'Evel Knievel syndrome' with traditional masculinity is obvious.

5 SENSATION-SEEKING

5	+	75	+	145	+
12	+	82	−	152	−
19	−	89	+	159	−
26	−	96	+	166	+
33	+	103	+	173	−
40	+	110	+	180	−
47	−	117	−	187	+
54	+	124	+	194	+
61	+	131	+	201	+
68	−	138	−	208	−

The sixth aspect of toughmindedness is dogmatism. High scorers have set, uncompromising views on most matters, and they are likely to defend them vigorously and vociferously. Low scorers are less rigid and less likely to see things in black and white; they are open to rational persuasion and very tolerant of uncertainty.

6 DOGMATISM

6	+	76	−	146	−
13	+	83	−	153	−
20	+	90	+	160	−
27	+	97	+	167	+
34	+	104	+	174	−
41	+	111	+	181	−
48	+	118	+	188	+
55	+	125	−	195	−
62	−	132	−	202	+
69	+	139	+	209	+

Whereas all of the above scales in this group of traits differentiate males and females to some extent, the final scale, called masculinity-femininity, focuses directly on items that have been found empirically to separate men from women. People scoring high on this factor are unconcerned about crawling insects, the sight of blood and other gruesome spectacles; they are tolerant of — and probably enjoy — violence, obscenity and swearing; they are disinclined to show weakness or sentimentality of any kind, for example by crying or expressing love, and rely on reason rather than intuition. Low scorers are easily upset by bugs, blood, brutality, etcetera, and have a high interest in delicate matters such as romance, children, fine arts, flowers and clothes. Obviously men score much higher on average than women, but there is also a great deal of variation within each sex. People whose scores resemble those typical of the opposite sex rather than their own are likely to have occupations atypical of their sex, but there is certainly no implication of homosexuality.

7 MASCULINITY-FEMININITY

7	+	77	+	147	−
14	−	84	−	154	+
21	−	91	−	161	−
28	−	98	−	168	+
35	−	105	−	175	+
42	−	112	+	182	−
49	−	119	−	189	−
56	+	126	+	196	+
63	+	133	−	203	−
70	−	140	−	210	+

Again, having obtained your seven scores, you may enter these on the profile sheet below and see whether you are generally 'tough' or 'tender'. If you find that your scores are mostly above the centre line, you are inclined to be tough; if they fall below, you are better described as a tender personality. We might have provided separate profile sheets for men and women (because men are characteristically more toughminded than women) but it is probably more interesting for people to discover this for themselves by looking at their own scores in relation to those of their friends and the population as a whole.

TOUGH-MINDEDNESS	AVERAGE	TENDER-MINDEDNESS
Aggressiveness	28 27 26 25 24 23 22 21 20 19 18 17 16 15 14 13 | 12 11 10 9 8 7 6 5 4 3 2 1 0	Peacefulness
Assertiveness	30 29 28 27 26 25 24 23 22 21 20 19 18 17 16 | 15 14 13 12 11 10 9 8 7 6 5 4 3 2 1 0	Submissiveness
Achievement-orientation	30 29 28 27 26 25 24 23 22 21 20 19 18 17 16 15 | 14 13 12 11 10 9 8 7 6 5 4 3 2 1 0	Unambitiousness
Manipulation	28 27 26 25 24 23 22 21 20 19 18 17 16 15 14 13 | 12 11 10 9 8 7 6 5 4 3 2 1 0	Empathy
Sensation-seeking	30 29 28 27 26 25 24 23 22 21 20 19 18 17 16 | 15 14 13 12 11 10 9 8 7 6 5 4 3 2 1 0	Unadventurousness
Dogmatism	30 29 28 27 26 25 24 23 22 21 20 19 18 17 16 15 | 14 13 12 11 10 9 8 7 6 5 4 3 2 1 0	Flexibility
Masculinity	27 26 25 24 23 22 21 20 19 18 17 16 15 14 13 12 | 11 10 9 8 7 6 5 4 3 2 1	Femininity

SENSE OF HUMOUR

The personality questionnaires given in the previous three chapters represent the direct 'self-report' approach to measuring personality. Their intention is fairly obvious and straightforward and they thus depend on the goodwill and cooperation of the subject. For most purposes this is quite a reasonable assumption, but as mentioned in Chapter 1, it is sometimes interesting and preferable to approach the testing of personality in a slightly more oblique and subtle way. One such indirect method is to study people's reactions to different types of jokes. Psychoanalysts have long regarded humour as a kind of window to the 'inner recesses' of the mind, and research psychologists have since teased out the actual links between enjoyment of different kinds of humour and personality type.

Before we describe these links, go ahead and complete the humour test below. It consists of 32 cartoons selected from various magazines and newspapers; hopefully the reader will not be familiar with too many of them. Work through the cartoons in order, making an immediate judgment as to how funny you think they are and assigning a rating of 1 to 5 to each according to this code:

> Not at all funny 1
> Slightly funny 2
> Moderately funny 3
> Very funny 4
> Extremely funny 5

To make scoring easier it is a good idea to mark your ratings on the table below. Remember to make your rating as soon as you 'get' the joke; do not ponder at it at length or come back to it later. If you don't see any joke in the cartoon after looking at it for a minute or so, give it a rating of 1 (equivalent to 'not at all funny').

Cartoon number	Your rating	Cartoon number	Your rating
1	. . . . . .	17	. . . . . .
2	. . . . . .	18	. . . . . .
3	. . . . . .	19	. . . . . .
4	. . . . . .	20	. . . . . .
5	. . . . . .	21	. . . . . .
6	. . . . . .	22	. . . . . .
7	. . . . . .	23	. . . . . .
8	. . . . . .	24	. . . . . .
9	. . . . . .	25	. . . . . .
10	. . . . . .	26	. . . . . .
11	. . . . . .	27	. . . . . .
12	. . . . . .	28	. . . . . .
13	. . . . . .	29	. . . . . .
14	. . . . . .	30	. . . . . .
15	. . . . . .	31	. . . . . .
16	. . . . . .	32	. . . . . .

"The game's up Farnsworth — are you coming quietly?"

2

"Would you mind repeating the question?"

3

"Well, I don't know ... but it might be fun to try!"

4

"I see Shabatakhta finally grabbed the tomb-lining contract."

5

"These belong to his cautious, rather groping,
formative period."

"I distinctly remember asking you not to do that."

7

"Leave the money on the table ...
leave the money on the table ..."

8

9

"Us they call 'the Fuzz'."

10

"Poor fools! You seem to forget, I have
the law on my side!"

||

"I have a little surprise for your birthday!"

12

NO
CARTOONS
ALLOWED
ON THIS
ISLAND.

rees.

13

"It's nearly time for us to do something spontaneous."

14

"Ah, here comes Edouard with the drinks now."

15

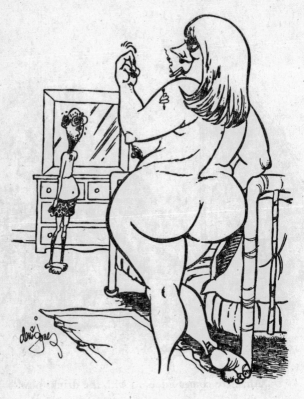

"Come here, Tiger !"

16

17

"As far as I know he just hits people with it."

18

"I understand you've sacked your gardener."

19

"George, please ... can't you wait until
we get back to the hotel?"

20

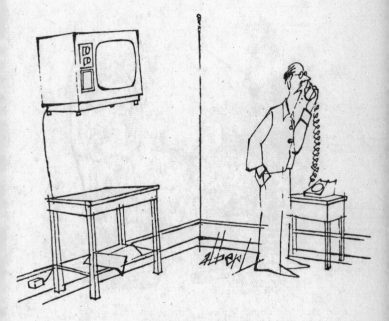

"It's the vertical hold."

21

"I'd like to tell my story my own way."

22

"Are you the person who called for an ambulance?"

23

"Can't a man have any PRIVACY?"

24

"Door !"

25

"Come into the Hospitality Room."

26

"I had hoped to bow out gracefully."

27

28

29

"I think this must be the obscene one, sergeant."

30

"I think that the split-second decision is
one of the chairman's main qualities."

31

"I want this wall just the colour of these
two little knobs!"

32

The cartoon test is scored for four categories of humour, and the first of these is called 'nonsense'. The nonsense cartoons are fairly devoid of any aggressive or sexual content; they are dependent for their effect mainly on their formal techniques — 'tricks' such as puns and incongruous combinations of elements. The eight jokes scored for this category are numbers 1, 5, 9, 13, 17, 21, 25 and 29. Simply add up the ratings you have given to these eight cartoons to give yourself a score somewhere between 8 and 40, and then mark your position on the profile sheet given below.

The second category of humour we have called 'satire'. This refers to jokes which involve the ridicule of certain persons, groups or institutions, a sort of indirect, interpersonal aggression. Cartoons 2, 6, 10, 14, 18, 22, 26 and 30 are scored on the satire scale; add your ratings as before.

The third category is one of more direct and 'pure' aggression. It includes cartoons depicting physical violence and brutality, outright insult, torture and sadism. Cartoons 3, 7, 11, 15, 19, 23, 27 and 31 are scored on this factor.

The fourth category of humour is probably the most obvious — it contains the explicitly sexual jokes. Indeed, some of them have been deliberately chosen to be as crude and vulgar as we thought would be permissible in a volume of this kind. Unfortunately, for the scale to discriminate effectively it was necessary that some people should be slightly offended by the content of these jokes. Cartoons 4, 8, 12, 16, 20, 24, 28 and 32 are scored (as above) on this sexual factor.

One final score may be calculated and entered on the profile sheet — this is quite simply a total of the other four scores, and represents a tendency to find jokes in general funny and to give them generous ratings. This cannot be taken as an indication that the high scorer has a 'good sense of humour' however; it could equally well be argued that such a person had indiscriminate taste. This test, like the preceding personality questionnaires, is intended only to describe people, not to evaluate them.

Now that you have drawn up your 'humour preference profile' you may wish to know how this is supposed to link up with personality. Briefly, extraverts tend to like sex jokes in particular, and outright aggression to some extent also; they are less fond of nonsense and satire but tend to give high ratings to jokes overall (showing a higher than average total score). Introverts, of course, show the reverse pattern; they dislike the blatantly libidinous sexual and aggressive jokes and prefer more cognitive types of humour such as nonsense and satire. Toughminded people frequently score high on aggression; tenderminded people usually dislike aggressive jokes. Emotional instability does not correlate clearly with any of the broad humour categories. Men are most different from women on the aggressive category (scoring higher on average); men also rate the sex jokes slightly higher than women and, because there is no gender effect with the other two categories (nonsense and satire), men normally come out with higher total scores. These relationships do not hold good for every individual case but they are true as generalizations — sufficiently true for researchers sometimes to use a humour test of this kind as a disguised index of personality.

	HIGH								AVERAGE								LOW							
Nonsense	30	29	28	27	26	25	24	23	22	21	20	19	18	17	16	15	14	13	12	11	10	9	8	7
Satire	30	29	28	27	26	25	24	23	22	21	20	19	18	17	16	15	14	13	12	11	10	9	8	7
Aggression	33	32	31	30	29	28	27	26	25	24	23	22	21	20	19	18	17	16	15	14	13	12	11	10
Sex	32	31	30	29	28	27	26	25	24	23	22	21	20	19	18	17	16	15	14	13	12	11	10	9
Total	125	121	117	113	109	105	101	97	93	89	85	81	77	73	69	65	61	57	53	49	45	41	37	33

6

SEX AND THE
AVERAGE WOMAN (OR MAN)

In no field of behaviour are there as many differences between people as in that of sex. It is possible to describe such behaviour in terms of average, but this is not very useful. Consider such an apparently simple question as the number of times that married people have intercourse. The usual answer given is 'Two or three times a week', and this is no doubt true—on the average. However, this average hides considerable individual differences, as well as differences due to such factors as age. Consider the following question and fill in your answer appropriately:

How frequently do you have sexual intercourse
with a member of the opposite sex?

1 More than once a day
2 Once a day
3 Four to six times a week
4 Two to three times a week
5 Once a week
6 Once a fortnight
7 Only rarely
8 Never

Figure 8 shows the distribution of answers given by a representative sample of the population, interviewed by a major polling organization in this country (Marplan). Clearly, there are enormous differences, even within a given age group; thus among the 20 year olds, some 'have sex' more than once a day, others only rarely or never. As people get older, they have intercourse less frequently, but the amount of variation remains large. Averages hide these differences between one person and another, and the same is true of attitudes towards sex; there too we find similar differences from one person to another, and averages do little to help us. Figures such as that given below may help in locating one's own position, in relation to other people; they do not, of course, tell us whether our own particular mode of behaviour is good, bad, or indifferent. Roughly speaking, the answer must be that factual information of this kind may be interesting, but it does not reflect in any way on the 'goodness' or otherwise of our conduct or our attitudes; because many people do a particular thing, or do it with a particular frequency, tells us nothing other than that this is what they do; it does not tell us whether their conduct is worthy of imitation, or of condemnation, or of indifference. We shall return to this point later.

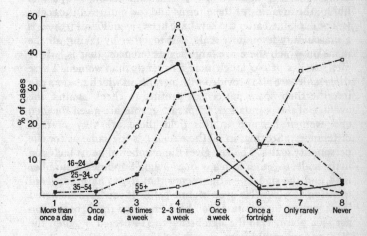

Figure 8

Sexual attitudes cover a lot of ground and there are many questionnaires in use which try to deal with the many questions raised. Below is given one which has had a great deal of work done on it, and to which the reactions of quite large numbers of people are known and have been analysed in detail. We shall first of all print the actual questionnaire, as it was used; not all of these questions have been used in the scales we shall be discussing, but most of them are so used, of course. The questionnaire should be filled in by the reader (either in the book or on a separate sheet of paper) and then scored by reference to the keys given. There is a discussion of the meaning of each of the scales and an indication is given of mean population scores so that readers can compare themselves with these standardization groups. Finally, we provide a graph with the various scales printed in such a way that the reader can fill in his own set of scores and obtain a profile relating it to the population averages. This should enable her/him to see at a glance on which scales she/he is above, below, or on a par with the majority of other people.

In addition to the eleven primary scales, we have two more complex scales, dealing with sexual satisfaction and sexual libido; the meaning of these terms and the nature of the scales will be explained after the keys have been given. Finally, there is a masculinity-femininity scale, put together by taking all the items on which there are large sex differences, that is, where men say 'Yes' or 'No' much more frequently than women. These three scales are also provided with a graph on which readers can inscribe their score pattern or profile, to check against the average of the population. (Separate graphs are given for men and women because in this field there are very marked differences.) Scoring, in all these scales, is the same as for the personality scales. The key gives the number of items included in the scale, together with a + or a − sign. Suppose the number is 14 and the sign a −; this means that if you have answered question 14 with a 'No', you get one point. If you have answered 'Yes', you get no points. If you have endorsed the '?' reply, you get ½ a point. Had the sign beside the 14 been a +, then the 'Yes' answer would have scored a point, the 'No' answer no points; the '?' would of course still rate ½ a point. In the questionnaire, some questions are worded slightly differently for men and women; these are marked M and F. Use the form of question appropriate to your sex.

Read each statement carefully, then record your answer as 'Yes' or 'No'. If you cannot decide, record a '?'. Please answer *every* question. There are no right or wrong answers. Don't think too long over each question; try to give an immediate answer which represents your *feeling* on each issue. Some questions are similar to others; there are good reasons for getting at the same attitude in slightly different ways.

Questionnaire

1   The opposite sex will respect you more if you are not too familiar with them. Yes ? No

2   Sex without love ('impersonal sex') is highly unsatisfactory. Agree ? Disagree

3   Conditions have to be just right to get me excited sexually. Yes ? No

4   All in all I am satisfied with my sex life. Yes ? No

5   Virginity is a girl's most valuable possession. Yes ? No

6   I think only rarely about sex. Agree ? Disagree

7   Sometimes it has been a problem to control my sex feelings. Yes ? No

8   Masturbation is unhealthy. Yes ? No

9   If I love a person I could do anything with them. Yes ? No

10 I get pleasant feelings from touching my sexual parts. Yes ? No

11 I have been deprived sexually Yes ? No

12 It is disgusting to see animals having sex relations in the street. Yes ? No

13 (M) I do not need to respect a woman, or love her, in order to enjoy petting and/or intercourse with her. Yes ? No

13 (F) I do not need to respect a man,
    or love him, in order to enjoy pet-
    ting and/or intercourse with him.   Yes ? No

14 I am sexually rather unattractive.   Yes ? No

15 Frankly, I prefer people of my own
    sex.   Yes ? No

16 Sex contacts have never been a
    problem to me.   True ? False

17 It is disturbing to see necking in
    public.   Yes ? No

18 Sexual feelings are sometimes un-
    pleasant to me.   True ? False

19 Something is lacking in my sex
    life.   Yes ? No

20 My sex behaviour has never
    caused me any trouble.   True ? False

21 My love life has been disappoint-
    ing.   Yes ? No

22 I never had many dates.   True ? False

23 I consciously try to keep sex
    thoughts out of my mind.   Yes ? No

24 I have felt guilty about sex experi-
    ences.   Yes ? No

25 It wouldn't bother me if the per-
    son I married were not a virgin.   True ? False

26 At times I have been afraid of my-
    self for what I might do sexually.   Yes ? No

27 I have had conflicts about my sex
    feelings towards a person of my
    own sex.   Yes ? No

28 I have many friends of the oppo-
    site sex.   Yes ? No

29 I have strong sex feelings but when I get a chance I can't seem to express myself.   Yes ? No

30 It doesn't take much to get me excited sexually.   True ? False

31 My parents' influence has inhibited me sexually.   Yes ? No

32 Thoughts about sex disturb me more than they should.   True ? False

33 People of my own sex frequently attract me.   Yes ? No

34 There are some things I wouldn't want to do with anyone.   True ? False

35 Children should be taught about sex.   Yes ? No

36 I understand homosexuals.   Yes ? No

37 I think about sex almost every day.   Yes ? No

38 One should not experiment with sex before marriage.   Agree ? Disagree

39 I get excited sexually very easily.   Yes ? No

40 The thought of a sex orgy is disgusting to me.   Yes ? No

41 It is better not to have sex relations until you are married.   True ? False

42 I find the thought of a coloured sex partner particularly exciting.   Yes ? No

43 I like to look at sexy pictures.   Yes ? No

44 My conscience bothers me too much.   Yes ? No

45 My religious beliefs are against sex.   Yes ? No

46 Sometimes sexual feelings overpower me.   Yes ? No

47 I feel nervous with the opposite sex.   Yes ? No

48 Sex thoughts drive me almost
    crazy.   Yes ? No

49 When I get excited I can think of
    nothing else but satisfaction.   Yes ? No

50 I feel at ease with people of the
    opposite sex.   Yes ? No

51 I don't like to be kissed.   True ? False

52 It is hard to talk with people of the
    opposite sex.   Yes ? No

53 I didn't learn the facts of life until I
    was quite old.   True ? False

54 I feel more comfortable when I am
    with my own sex.   Yes ? No

55 I enjoy petting.   Yes ? No

56 I worry a lot about sex.   Yes ? No

57 The Pill should be universally
    available.   Yes ? No

58 Seeing a person nude doesn't inter-
    est me.   True ? False

59 Sometimes thinking about sex
    makes me very nervous.   Yes ? No

60 Perverted thoughts have some-
    times bothered me.   Yes ? No

61 I am embarrassed to talk about sex.   Yes ? No

62 Young people should learn about
    sex through their own experience.   Yes ? No

63 Sometimes the woman should be
    sexually aggressive.   Yes ? No

64 Sex jokes disgust me.   Yes ? No

65 I believe in taking my pleasures where I find them.   Yes ? No

66 A person should learn about sex gradually by experimenting with it.   Yes ? No

67 Young people should be allowed out at night without being too closely checked.   Yes ? No

68 I have sometimes felt like humiliating my sex partner.   Yes ? No

69 I would particularly protect my children from contacts with sex.   Yes ? No

70 Self-relief is not dangerous as long as it is done in a healthy way.   Yes ? No

71 (M) I get very excited when touching a woman's breasts.   Yes ? No

71 (F) I get very excited when men touch my breasts.   Yes ? No

72 I have been involved with more than one sex affair at the same time.   Yes ? No

73 Homosexuality is normal for some people.   Yes ? No

74 It is alright to seduce a person who is old enough to know what they are doing.   Yes ? No

75 I have sometimes felt hostile to my sex partner.   Yes ? No

76 I like to look at pictures of nudes.   Yes ? No

77 If I had the chance to see people making love, without being seen, I would take it.   Yes ? No

78 Pornographic writings should be
    freely allowed to be published.   Yes ? No

79 Prostitution should be legally per-
    mitted.   Yes ? No

80 Decisions about abortion should
    be the concern of no one but the
    woman concerned.   Yes ? No

81 There are too many immoral plays
    on TV.   Yes ? No

82 The dual standard of morality,
    allowing men greater freedom, is
    natural and should be continued.   Yes ? No

83 We should do away with marriage
    entirely.   Yes ? No

84 I had some bad sex experiences
    when I was young.   Yes ? No

85 There should be no censorship, on
    sexual grounds, of plays and films. Agree ? Disagree

86 Sex is far and away my greatest
    pleasure.   Yes ? No

87 Sexual permissiveness threatens to
    undermine the entire foundation
    of civilized society.   Yes ? No

88 Sex should be used only for the
    purpose of reproduction, not for
    personal pleasure.   True ? False

89 Absolute faithfulness to one part-
    ner throughout life is nearly as silly
    as celibacy.   Yes ? No

90 I prefer to have intercourse under
    the bedcovers and with the light
    off.   Yes ? No

91 The present preoccupation with sex in our society has been largely created by films, newspapers, television and advertising.   True ? False

92 I would enjoy watching my usual partner having intercourse with someone else.   Yes ? No

93 Sex play amongst young children is quite harmless.   Yes ? No

94 Females do not have such strong sexual desire as males.   True ? False

95 I would vote for a law which permitted polygamy.   Yes ? No

96 Even though one is having regular intercourse, masturbation is good for a change.   Yes ? No

97 I would prefer to have a new sex partner every night.   Yes ? No

98 I only get sexually aroused at night; never in the daytime.   Yes ? No

99 I prefer partners who are several years older than myself.   Yes ? No

100 My sexual fancies often involve flogging.   Yes ? No

101 I make lots of vocal noises during intercourse.   Yes ? No

102 Sex is more exciting with a stranger.   Yes ? No

103 I could never discuss sex with my parents.   True ? False

104 There are some things I only do to please my sex partner.   True ? False

105 I don't always know for sure when

I have had an orgasm.   True ? False

106 To me few things are more impor-
tant than sex.   True ? False

107 I am very keen on babies.   Yes ? No

108 My sex partner satisfies all my phy-
sical needs completely.   Yes ? No

109 Sex is not all that important to me. True ? False

110 Most men are sex mad.   True ? False

111 Being good in bed is terribly im-
portant to my marriage partner.   Yes ? No

112 I enjoy very lengthy pre-coital love
play.   Yes ? No

113 (M) I find it easy to tell my sex partner what I like or I don't like
about her love-making.   Yes ? No

113 (F) I find I easy to tell my sex partner what I like or don't like about
his love-making.   Yes ? No

114 I would like my sex partner to be
more expert and experienced.   Yes ? No

115 To me, psychological factors in my
sex partner are more important
than physical ones.   Yes ? No

116 I sometimes feel like scratching
and biting my partner during
intercourse.   Yes ? No

117 No one has ever been able to satisfy
me sexually.   True ? False

118 I feel sexually less competent than
my friends.   Yes ? No

119 Group sex appeals to me.   Yes ? No

120 The thought of an illicit relationship excites me.   Yes ? No

121 I usually feel aggressive with my
sexual partner.   Yes ? No

122 I believe my sexual activities are
average.   Yes ? No

123 It disturbs me to look at sexy photographs.   Yes ? No

124 I am afraid of sexual relationships.   Yes ? No

125 (M) I often wish that women would
be more forthcoming sexually.   Yes ? No

125 (F) I often wish that men would be
less demanding sexually.   Yes ? No

126 I can't stand people touching me.   True ? False

127 Physical sex is the most important
part of marriage.   Yes ? No

128 I prefer my partner to dictate the
rules of the sexual game.   Yes ? No

129 I find 'straight sex' unsatisfactory. True ? False

130 I always make love in the nude.   Yes ? No

131 Physical attraction is extremely
important to me.   Yes ? No

132 In a sexual union, tenderness is the
most important quality.   Yes ? No

133 (M) Female genitals are aestheti-
cally unpleasing.   Agree ? Disagree

133 (F) Male genitals are aesthetically
unpleasing.   Agree ? Disagree

134 I object to four-letter swear words
being used in mixed company.   Yes ? No

135 The idea of 'wife swapping' is
extremely distasteful to me.   True   ?   False

136 Romantic love is just puerile illu-
sion.   Yes   ?   No

137 The need for birth control upsets
my love-making because it makes
everything so cold-blooded and
planned.   Yes   ?   No

138 I love physical contact with mem-
bers of the opposite sex.   Yes   ?   No

139 (M) I cannot discuss sexual matters
with my wife (or habitual sex part-
ner).   True   ?   False

139 (F) I cannot discuss sexual matters
with my husband (or habitual sex
partner).   True   ?   False

140 People who attend 'strip-tease'
shows are sexually abnormal.   Yes   ?   No

141 The naked human body is a pleas-
ing sight.   Yes   ?   No

142 I can take sex and I can leave it
alone.   True   ?   False

143 I think taking the Pill for any
length of time is dangerous to a
woman's health.   Yes   ?   No

144 (M) It would not disturb me over-
much if my sex partner had sexual
relations with someone else, as
long as she returned to me.   True   ?   False

144 (F) It would not disturb me over-
much if my sex partner had sexual
relations with someone else, as
long as he returned to me.   True   ?   False

145 (M) Men are more selfish in their
love-making than women.   Yes ? No

145 (F) Women are more selfish in
their love-making than men.   Yes ? No

146 Some forms of love-making are disgusting to me.   Yes ? No

147 It is right that the man should be
the dominant partner in a sex rela-
tionship.   Yes ? No

148 Women often use sex to gain all
sorts of advantages.   Yes ? No

149 The reading of 'girlie' magazines
suggests failure to achieve adult
attitudes to sex.   Yes ? No

150 In matters of sex, women always
seem to come off second-best.   Yes ? No

151 If you were invited to see a 'blue' film would you:
      (a) Accept   (b) Refuse

152 If you were offered a highly pornographic book,
would you:
      (a) Accept it   (b) Reject it

153 If you were invited to take part in an orgy, would you:
      (a) Take part   (b) Refuse

154 Ideally, would you prefer to have intercourse:
      (a) Never   (e) 3-5 times a week
      (b) Once a month   (f) Every day
      (c) Once a week   (g) More than once a day
      (d) Twice a week

155 (M) Have you ever suffered from impotence:
      (a) Never   (d) Often
      (b) Once or twice   (e) More often than not
      (c) Several times   (f) Always

155 (F) Have you ever suffered from frigidity:
        (a) Never   (d) Often
        (b) Once or twice (e) More often than not
        (c) Several times (f) Always

156 (M) Have you ever suffered from ejaculatio praecox
      (premature ejaculation)?
        (a) Very often   (d) Not very often
        (b) Often   (e) Hardly ever
        (c) Middling   (f) Never

156 (F) Do you usually have orgasm during intercourse:
        (a) Very often   (d) Not very often
        (b) Often   (e) Hardly ever
        (c) Middling   (f) Never

157 At what age did you have your first intercourse?
    (If virgin, leave blank.)

158 Rate the habitual strength of your sexual desire from 10
(absolutely overwhelming and all-embracing) to 1 (very
weak and almost non-existent).

159 Rate the strength of the influences which inhibit you sexually (moral, aesthetic, religious, etcetera) from 10
(terribly strong, completely inhibiting) to 1 (very weak and
almost non-existent).

Our first scale is one of permissiveness and a high score on this scale means that you have modern, trendy, permissive attitudes to sex and are opposed to religious, Victorian, 'old-fashioned' views of what is right and proper in sexual affairs. You aren't bothered about virginity, favour pre-marital (or even extra-marital) sex, believe that birth control should be universally available and generally regard sex as a pleasurable activity that is nobody's concern but that of the 'consenting adults' (or adolescents — possibly even children) involved. A low score on the scale means exactly the opposite; a person with a low score takes sexual intercourse much more seriously, has regard to the marriage vows, and is not in favour of 'immorality' in any shape or form. Intermediate scores, of course, indicate an attitude not going to either extreme. Below is given the key to this scale.

1 PERMISSIVENESS

5 −	57 +	85 +
17 −	64 −	87 −
25 +	78 +	93 +
38 −	79 +	134 −
41 −	81 −	

Our second scale deals with sexual fulfilment, or the general satisfaction a person derives from his sex life at the present time. High scores indicate considerable fulfilment, low scores lack of fulfilment. Satisfaction with one's sex life is naturally for most people a very desirable state of affairs, and low scores on this scale indicate considerable unhappiness and dissatisfaction. There are different causes for dissatisfaction, of course, and a study of the individual items will reveal some of the particular causes active for a particular person. These causes may lie in the person herself or himself, or they may lie in the partner; what can be done to achieve a happier state of affairs depends in large measure on the precise constellation of causes involved. Below is given the key to this scale.

2 FULFILMENT

4	+	20	+	113	+
11	−	21	−	114	−
16	+	56	−	118	−
19	−	108	+	139	−

Dissatisfaction with one's sex life often leads to neurotic sexual reactions — using the term 'neurotic' not in the psychiatric sense of mental abnormality, but in the more common-parlance one of indicating some unbalance or dysfunction in one's life and behaviour. People scoring high on this scale are obviously having trouble with their sex life; they find it difficult to control their impulses, or to act them out; they are easily disturbed or upset by their own thoughts and actions; they worry about sexual matters, and thus make them worse. People with very high scores on this scale might consider going to see their doctor, or seek advice elsewhere. The scoring key is as follows.

3 NEUROTIC SEX

7	+	26	+	59	+
18	+	32	+	60	+
20	+	44	+	84	+
23	+	46	+		
24	+	56	+		

The fourth scale is concerned with impersonal sex, that is, the tendency to regard the sex partner simply as a sex object, and pay no attention to his or her personality, individual temperament or character, and in particular to seek only sensual satisfaction rather than try to enter into a meaningful personal relationship. Inevitably men have higher scores on this scale than women; impersonal sex is not entirely reserved for men, but women tend to regard this form of sexual behaviour as much less attractive than do men. The key for this scale is given below.

4 IMPERSONAL SEX

2	−	92	+	120	+
40	−	95	+	135	−
65	+	97	+	144	+
83	+	102	+	153	+ (a)
89	+	119	+		

Scale 5 deals with pornography, that is, the liking for the pictorial or verbal description of sexual scenes, usually in as explicit a manner as can be procured. Such voyeuristic activities as seeing other people make love also come into this scale. The many current debates on sex films, on the television screen and in the theatre deal essentially with the questions here asked; a high score indicates a liking (or at least a considerable tolerance) for pornographic material, while a low score shows disapproval and intolerance.

5 PORNOGRAPHY

10	+	76	+	151	+ (a)
43	+	77	+	152	+ (a)
58	−	141	+		

The sixth scale, sexual shyness, is self-explanatory; persons with high scores feel nervous with the opposite sex, are nervous and embarrassed when talking about sex, and are even sometimes afraid of sexual relationships altogether. High scores indicate a marked degree of this reluctance to enter into sexual relationships, while low scores indicate a more 'normal' sort of reaction. The key for this scale is given below.

6 SEXUAL SHYNESS

47 +	52 +	61 +
50 −	59 +	124 +

The seventh scale, entitled 'prudishness', is in some degree similar to the preceding one, and the name explains quite well what the scale is all about. People with high scores withdraw from even mild manifestations of sexual passion, and don't like to think of love-making or indulge in it. Again, low scores are more normal and usual, high scores somewhat unusual. The key to this scale is given below.

7 PRUDISHNESS

51 +	64 +	122 −
55 −	71 −	126 +
58 +	112 −	141 −

Scale eight, sexual disgust, is a rather stronger expression of the same sentiment as scale seven, prudishness; a person with a high score reacts with disgust to some forms of love-making, even when loving the usual sex partner, and cannot bring her or himself to take part in such activities. The person with a high score easily reacts with disgust to sexual behaviour which, to many other people, is quite normal; a low score indicates a rather more robust reaction potential. The key to this scale is given below.

8 SEXUAL DISGUST

9	–	104	+	133	+
34	+	112	–	146	+

Sexual excitement or ease of arousal constitutes our ninth scale. For some people, conditions have to be just right in order for them to react with sexual arousal; such persons would have low scores on this scale. Others get sexually excited very easily; they would have high scores. As one might have expected, people with high scores on the three preceding scales tend to have low scores on this scale. The key is given below.

9 SEXUAL EXCITEMENT

3	–	30	+	39	+
6	–	34	–	71	+
9	+	37	+	146	–

Physical sex, the tenth scale, indicates a stress on the physical side of love, and a passionate longing for the actual physical act of intercourse. For people high on this scale, being good in bed is terribly important in a partner; more so, perhaps, than other, more spiritual qualities which low scorers might look for in preference. High scorers value sex above most other things, and specifically lay emphasis on intercourse, to the exclusion of other aspects of a loving relationship. The key to this scale is given below.

10 PHYSICAL SEX

31	–	86	+	111	+
48	+	106	+	127	+
49	+	109	–	131	+
71	+				

The last of the simple scales deals with aggressive sex; here the emphasis is on hostility in the sexual relationship, on subjugating the partner, and possibly humiliating her or him. It is idle to pretend that such thoughts and feelings do not often enter into sexual relationships; for some people, they are more likely to occur than for others, and high scorers clearly are more prone to hostile, aggressive impulses toward their partners. The key to this scale is given below.

11 AGGRESSIVE SEX

68	+	101	+	121	+
75	+	116	+	132	–

		HIGH	AVERAGE	LOW
Permissiveness		14 13 12 11 10	9 8 7 6 5 4 3	
Fulfilment		12 11 10 9 8	7 6 5 4 3 2	
Neurotic sex		9 8 7 6 5 4	3 2 1 0	
Impersonal sex	M	12 11 10 9 8	7 6 5 4 3 2 1	
	F	9 8 7 6 5 4	3 2 1 0	
Pornography	M	8 7 6 5	4 3 2 1 0	
	F	8 7 6 5 4	3 2 1 0	
Sexual shyness		6 5 4 3 2	1	0
Prudishness		8 7 6 5 4 3 2	1	0
Sexual disgust		6 5 4 3	2	1 0
Sexual excitement	M	9 8 7 6	5 4 3 2 1	
	F	9 8 7 6 5	4 3 2 1 0	
Physical sex		9 8 7 6 5 4	3	2 1 0
Aggressive sex		6 5 4 3	2	1 0

We next come to two 'superscales', that is, scales which are built on the relationships obtaining between the simple scales we have so far discussed. Obviously, there are correlations between permissiveness, sexual excitement, pornography, impersonal sex and physical sex; we can say that a person who has high scores on all or most of these scales has a strong sexual libido; in other words, he has a strong sex drive. Our *sexual libido* scale attempts to measure the strength of a person's sex drive; the key to this scale is given below. In a similar manner, it is intuitively clear that the fulfilment scale would correlate negatively with the scales of neurotic sex, sexual shyness, prudishness, and sexual disgust; we have called this combined scale one of *sexual satisfaction*, and again the key is supplied below. It is interesting to note that in large samples of the population we have repeatedly found that sexual libido and sexual satisfaction are quite uncorrelated; in other words, a person's satisfaction with her or his sex life is quite independent of her or his sexual appetite. People can lead perfectly satisfactory sex lives when they lay a minimum of stress on active, energetic, frequent love-making, and they can lead perfectly satisfactory sex lives when such active, energetic, frequent love-making is almost their only, and certainly their main, aim in life. It is always difficult to persuade people of one kind that others, differing so much from them in this respect, may nevertheless not only prefer their own mode of adjustment but prosper and be happy with it. Yet so it is. There are many different ways of achieving happiness, and frequency of intercourse is not the only way of producing a satisfactory sexual relationship!

SEXUAL LIBIDO

1	–	43	+	89	+
2	–	46	+	92	+
5	–	65	+	95	+
6	–	72	+	96	+
10	+	74	+	119	+
25	+	76	+	120	+
37	+	77	+	134	–
38	–	78	+	135	–
39	+	79	+	151	+ (a)
40	–	81	–	152	+ (a)
41	–	85	+	153	+ (a)
42	+	87	–	154	+ (efg)

SEXUAL SATISFACTION

4	+	21	–	108	+
11	–	31	–	117	–
15	–	32	–	118	–
18	–	44	–	124	–
19	–	56	–	133	–
20	+				

Our last scale is the masculinity-femininity scale, constructed as
explained already by choosing items which are endorsed much
more frequently by one sex or the other. By 'masculinity' we
here mean nothing other than that high scores on the scale
indicate that the reader agrees with the typical male in our
society about sexual matters and disagrees with the typical
female; whether this makes him (or her!) a male chauvinist pig,
we leave to the reader to judge. By 'femininity', similarly, we
mean nothing beyond the fact that the low-scoring reader (male
or female) tends to agree with females rather than with males on
questions of sexual behaviour. It follows from the construction
of the scale that women may have 'masculine' scores, or men
'feminine' ones; this does not reflect on their masculinity or
femininity as ordinarily understood and certainly has no
implications of homosexuality or lesbianism.

MASCULINITY-FEMININITY

2	–	63	+	96	+
3	–	64	–	97	+
7	+	65	+	101	–
10	+	67	+	102	+
13	+	69	–	106	+
16	–	76	+	109	–
18	–	77	+	113	+
22	+	78	+	114	–
30	+	79	+	116	–
37	+	80	–	119	+
39	+	84	–	120	+
40	–	85	+	128	–
42	+	86	+	135	–
43	+	89	+	145	+
44	–	91	–	146	–
55	+	92	+	147	–
58	–	95	+		

	HIGH	AVERAGE	LOW
Sexual Libido — M	34 32 30 28 26 24	22	20 18 16 14 12 10 8
Sexual Libido — F	29 27 25 23 21 19	17	15 13 11 9 7 5 3
Sexual Satisfaction — M	16 15 14 13 12	11	10 9 8 7 6 5 4
Sexual Satisfaction — F	16 15 14 13 12	11	10 9 8 7 6 5 4
Masculinity — M	48 45 42 39 36	33	30 27 24 21 18 15 12
Femininity — F	42 39 36 33 30 27	24	21 18 15 12 9 6 3

7

SOCIAL AND POLITICAL ATTITUDES

The questionnaire given in the last chapter deals specifically with attitudes in the field of sex. We now consider attitudes which cover the whole spectrum of social and political controversy. Below are given 176 statements which represent widely-held opinions on various social questions, selected from speeches, books, newspapers and other sources. They were chosen in such a way that most people are likely to agree with some and to disagree with others.

For each statement, record your personal opinion regarding it. Use the following system of marking:

+ +   if you strongly agree with the statement
+   if you agree on the whole
0   if you can't decide for or against, or if you think the question is worded in such a way that you can't give an answer
—   if you disagree on the whole
— — if you strongly disagree

Answer frankly. The answer required is your own personal opinion. Do not consult any other person while you are giving your answers.

Opinion statements   *Your opinion*

1   Few people really know what is in their own best   . . . .
     interests in the long run.

2   We should stop trying to play a world role be-
     yond our strength.   . . . .

3   War can never be justified even if it seems the
     only way to protect our national rights and
     honour.   ....

4   There is no survival of any kind after death.   ....

5   It would be best to keep coloured people in
     their own districts and schools, in order to pre-
     vent too much contact with whites.   ....

6   No one should be allowed to buy privileges in
     education or medical care for his family.   ....

7   Blood sports, like fox hunting for instance, are
     vicious and cruel, and should be forbidden.   ....

8   It is only by returning to our glorious and forgot-
     ten past that real social progress can be made.   ....

9   More severe punishment of criminals will reduce
     crime.   ....

10   Homosexuals are not criminals and should never
     be treated as such.   ....

11   The minority should be free to criticise majority
     decisions.   ....

12   The people of Africa should be left to fend for
     themselves.   .....

13   Compulsory military training in peace-time is
     essential for the survival of this country.   ....

14   The Church should attempt to increase its influ-
     ence on the life of the nation.   ....

15   There is no such thing as a 'class struggle' in this
     country today.   ....

16   Too much is paid in tax by people with high
     incomes.   ....

17   There is no harm in travelling occasionally with-
     out a ticket, if you can get away with.it.   ....

18   National minorities should have the right
     to govern themselves   ....

19   Criminal violence should be punished more severe-
     ly than just by imprisonment.   ....

20   The government is gradually taking away our
     basic freedom.   ....

21   People suffering from incurable diseases should
     have the choice of being put painlessly to death.   ....

22   The evils of war are greater than any conceivable
     benefits.   ....

23   Most religious people are hypocrites.   ....

24   True democracy is limited in this country because
     of the special privileges enjoyed by business and
     industry.   ....

25   It is clearly unfair that many people should ac-
     quire large incomes, not through work but
     through inheritance.   ....

26   Men are not created equal; it is obvious that some
     are better than others.   ....

27   To compromise with our political opponents is
     dangerous because it usually leads to letting down
     our own side.   ....

28   The laws against 'soft' drugs like marijuana are
     too strict.   ....

29   The government is spending too much money on
     social welfare and education.   ....

30   It is just as well that the struggle of life tends to
     weed out those who cannot stand the pace.   ....

31   Most labour troubles are due to the work of radi-
     cal agitators.   ....

32   Life in the old days used to be much more plea-
     sant than nowadays.   ....

33 The church is the main bulwark opposing the evil
    trends of modern society.   ....

34 Capitalism has worked well in this country and
    should not be changed.   ....

35 'Free enterprise' is another way of saying 'exploi-
    tation of the workers'.   ....

36 Life is so short that a man is justified in enjoying
    himself as much as he can.   ....

37 A group which allows too much difference of
    opinion amongst its members cannot last long.   ....

38 Picasso and other modern painters are in no way
    inferior to past masters like Rembrandt or Titian.   ....

39 Industrial depressions can be prevented by proper
    government planning.   ....

40 Persons with serious hereditary defects and dis-
    orders should be compulsorily sterilized.   ....

41 A classless society is impossible.   ....

42 Modern students show unrest because the old
    ways have failed.   ....

43 Religious beliefs of all kinds are just superstitions.   ....

44 Ultimately private property should be abolished
    and complete socialism introduced.   ....

45 Most of the countries which have received econo-
    mic help from us end up resenting what we have
    done for them.   ....

46 The greatest threats to this country during the
    last fifty years have come from foreign ideas and
    agitators.   ....

47 Any formal international government is impos-
    sible.   ....

48 Men and women have the right to find out whether they are sexually suited before marriage (e.g. by trial marriage). . . . .

49 It is better to stick by what you have than to be trying new things you don't really know about. . . . .

50 The universe was created by God. . . . .

51 Production and trade should be free from government interference. . . . .

52 Speculators and financiers have been responsible very largely for our economic difficulties. . . . .

53 Strikes should be made illegal. . . . .

54 Royalty and nobility encourage snobbishness in a country, and are not compatible with democracy. . . . .

55 In strikes and disputes between workers and employers I usually side with the workers . . . .

56 Our country is probably no better than many others. . . . .

57 Birth control, except when recommended by a doctor, should always be illegal. . . . .

58 Tradition has too big an influence in this country. . . . .

59 Coloured people are innately inferior to white people. . . . .

60 In practice the rich and the poor are not equal before the law. . . . .

61 Improving slum areas is a waste of money. . . . .

62 War is inherent in human nature. . . . .

63 Equal pay for equal work is long overdue; present arrangements are unfair to women workers. . . .

64 An impartial body should fix the wages of the workers, and control prices. . . . .

65 In the interest of peace, we must give up part of
    our national sovereignty.   ....

66 Divorce laws should be altered to make divorce
    easier.   ....

67 Children today need more discipline.   ....

68 Jews are as valuable citizens as any other group.   ....

69 There exists a class of people whose family back-
    ground and traditions make them most fitted to
    lead the country.   ....

70 Political extremists must have the right to advo-
    cate their beliefs.   ....

71 The 'new look' in drama and TV plays is an im-
    provement on the old-fashioned type of entertain-
    ment.   ....

72 No society can be called civilized which does not
    have some formal national health service, paid
    largely from taxes.   ....

73 Many politicians are bought off by some private
    interest.   ....

74 It is wrong to punish a man who helps another
    country because he prefers it to his own.   ....

75 Sexual immorality destroys the marriage rela-
    tion, which is the basis of our civilization.   ....

76 The 'free-and-easy' play-way of teaching young-
    sters results in poor reading and writing.   ....

77 It would be a mistake to have coloured people as
    foremen over whites.   ....

78 In this country it is big business that controls the
    state, not the people in general.   ....

79 Control of inflation is more important than a low
    rate of unemployment.   ....

80   Permissiveness in our society has gone much too
     far.   . . . .

81   Most politicians don't seem to me to really mean
     what they say.   . . . .

82   'My country right or wrong' is a saying which ex-
     presses a fundamentally desirable attitude.   . . . .

83   We spend too little on our armed forces.   . . . .

84   We should recognise that we have duties to society
     as well as rights.   . . . .

85   Negroes may be behind white people in many
     areas of achievement, but there is definitely no
     difference between the two races in basic intelli-
     gence.   . . . .

86   All social planning leads to human regimentation. . . . .

87   The sight of young men with beards and long hair
     is unpleasant.   . . . .

88   The welfare state gives too much help to people
     who refuse to do a proper day's work.   . . . .

89   Our treatment of criminals is too harsh; we should
     try to cure them, not punish them.   . . . .

90   It will always be necessary to have a few strong,
     able people actually running everything.   . . . .

91   The United Nations Organisation is useless and
     does not deserve our support.   . . . .

92   Pacifism is simply not a practical philosophy in
     the world today.   . . . .

93   The idea of God is an invention of the human
     mind.   . . . .

94   We should not restrict immigration into this
     country as much as we have done in the past.   . . . .

95   Private profit is the main motive for hard work. . . . .

96   There is very little discipline in today's youth.   ....

97   It is the moral responsibility of strong nations to
      protect and develop weaker and poorer nations.   ....

98   Sex crimes, such as rape and attacks on children,
      deserve more than mere imprisonment; such
      criminals ought to be flogged or worse.   ....

99   Communists should not be allowed to hold jobs in
      government service.   ....

100   We spend too little money on foreign aid.   ....

101   An occupation by a foreign power is better than
      war.   ....

102   The average man can live a good enough life with-
      out religion.   ....

103   In capitalist countries there is an inevitable con-
      flict between workers and employers.   ....

104   Great wealth should be shared much more than
      at present.   ....

105   A white lie is often a good thing.   ....

106   The great increase in drug taking by the young is
      another example of how far our society has deter-
      iorated.   ....

107   The death penalty is barbaric, and its abolition
      right and proper.   ....

108   The police should have the right to listen in on
      private telephone conversations when investiga-
      ting crime.   ....

109   The so-called underdog deserves little sympathy
      or help from successful people.   ....

110   We have never, as a nation, fought an unjust war.   ....

111   We should believe without question all that we
      are taught by the Church.   ....

112 In this country, the most able rise to the top.   ....

113 A firm should produce what is most profitable, not what the government believes to be in the national interest.   ....

114 The practical man is of more use to society than the thinker.   ...

115 Even though the masses behave pretty stupidly at times, I have a lot of faith in the common sense of the ordinary man.   ....

116 The maintenance of internal order within the nation is more important than ensuring that there is complete freedom for all.   ....

117 Poverty, mental illness and other problems are a responsibility for the whole community.   ....

118 The dropping of the first atom bomb on a Japanese city, killing thousands of innocent women and children, was morally wrong and incompatible with our kind of civilization.   ....

119 Life is not perfect nowadays but it is much better than it used to be.   ....

120 Sunday observance is old-fashioned and should cease to govern our behaviour.   ....

121 Capitalism is immoral because it exploits the worker by failing to give him full value for his productive labour.   ....

122 Nowadays, more and more people are prying into matters which do not concern them.   ....

123 There are many advantages to having a Queen or King to govern the country, provided they do not have too much power.   ....

124 Most modern art is pretentious nonsense.   ....

125 The 'welfare state' tends to destroy individual initiative.   ....

126 A person should be free to take his own life, if he
wishes to do so without any interference from
society.   ....

127 On the whole, workers in this country are fairly
treated by their employers.   ....

128 If you start trying to change things very much,
you usually make them worse.   ....

129 Christ was divine, wholly or partly, in a sense different from other men.   ....

130 The nationalisation of the great industries is
likely to lead to inefficiency, bureaucracy and
stagnation.   ....

131 People should realise that their greatest obligation
is to their family.   ....

132 Business competition is necessary for national
welfare.   ....

133 Most strikes are caused by bad management.   ....

134 We ought to have a world government to guarantee the welfare of all nations irrespective of the
rights of any nation.   ....

135 Sex relations except in marriage are always wrong.   ....

136 The way wealth is distributed at the moment is
unsound and unjust.   ....

137 It is always a good idea to look for new ways of
doing things.   ....

138 There are no such things as 'supernatural powers'.   ....

139 Economic security for all is impossible under capitalism.   ....

140 The less government the better.   ....

141 There are many responsible positions for which women are unsuited, such as judgeships, ministerial office and high positions in banking and industry.   . . . .

142 Trade unions do more harm than good to industrial progress.   . . . .

143 I would support my country even against my convictions.   . . . .

144 Free love between men and women should be encouraged as a means towards mental and physical health.   . . . .

145 Scientific inventions have carried us too far too fast; we should be given a resting pause now.   . . . .

146 Government nowadays is too centralised.   . . . .

147 Negroes are often denied opportunities for good jobs and promotions that are given to white people.   . . . .

148 Our nation is more democratic than any other nation.   . . . .

149 Housing will never be adequate until the government acquires ownership of all land.   . . . .

150 It is wrong that men should be permitted greater sexual freedom than women by society.   . . . .

151 The government should do a lot more to regulate the activities of labour unions.   . . . .

152 In taking part in any form of world organisation, this country should make certain that none of its independence and power is lost.   . . . .

153 The practice of birth control should be discouraged.   . . . .

154 Modern adolescents are no more immoral than were their parents or grandparents at their age.   . . . .

155 There may be a few exceptions, but in general
Jews are pretty much alike.   . . . .

156 Workers should take part in the running of busi-
nesses in which they are employed.   . . . .

157 Women are not really the equals of men and
never will be.   . . . .

158 Teachers have no business to take an active part
in politics.   . . . .

159 Censorship of books and films should be comple-
tely abolished.   . . . .

160 A national health service does not give doctors an
opportunity to do their best for their patients.   . . . .

161 Most politicians can be trusted to do what they
think is best for the country.   . . . .

162 Conscientious objectors are traitors to their country and should be treated accordingly.   . . . .

163 The laws restricting abortion should be abolished.   . . . .

164 The permissive modern ways of bringing up children are an improvement on older methods.   . . . .

165 All kinds of discrimination against the coloured
races, the Jews, etcetera, should be illegal and
subject to heavy penalties.   . . . .

166 Democracy depends fundamentally on the exis-
tence of free business enterprise.   . . . .

167 Slumps and unemployment are the inevitable consequences of capitalism.   . . . .

168 The government must ensure *above everything
else* that unemployment is kept very low.   . . . .

169 The school leaving age should be raised as much
as possible, whether young people want to stay on
or not.   . . . .

170 It seems to me that whoever you vote for, things
   go on pretty much the same.   . . . .

171 This country is just as selfish as any other nation.   . . . .

172 In the interest of peace, the private manufacture
   of arms and ammunition must be abolished.   . . . .

173 The nation exists for the benefit of the individual,
   not the individual for the benefit of the nation.   . . . .

174 When it comes to the things that count, all races
   are certainly not equal.   . . . .

175 Stable peace will only be possible in a socialist
   world.   . . . .

176 Morals in this country are pretty bad, and getting
   worse.   . . . .

This questionnaire may be scored for a number of primary or
'content' factors, and the first of these is permissiveness. High
scorers have favourable attitudes towards sexual freedom,
drug-taking, and 'freaky' people such as hippies and homosexuals. Generally, they adopt an easy-going, tolerant and
hedonistic philosophy of life. Low scorers have a strong distaste
for all these things and favour strict censorship, legal control of
the so-called vices, and severe punishments for offenders. Not
surprisingly, this permissiveness factor correlates highly with
the permissiveness factor derived from the sexual attitudes
questionnaire above.

The key for the permissiveness scale is given below. This, and
the other keys provided in this chapter, are somewhat more
complicated than those given for the previous questionnaires. If
the sign after the question number is positive, a + + answer is
scored 5, + scores 4, 0 scores 3, — scores 2 and — — scores 1. If
the sign after the question number is a minus then the whole
five-point scale is reversed: — — is scored 5, — scores 4, 0 scores
3, + scores 2 and + + scores 1. The principle is the same as
before but we are now using a five-point scale with a range of 1
to 5 on each item instead of a three-point scale with a range of 0
to 1. Now here is the key.

1 PERMISSIVENESS

9	—	75	—	126	+
10	+	76	—	131	—
17	+	80	—	135	—
28	+	87	—	144	+
42	+	89	+	153	—
48	+	96	—	154	+
57	—	98	—	159	+
66	+	106	—	163	+
67	—	107	+	164	+
71	+	124	—	176	—

The second attitude factor is called racism. High scorers are opposed to coloured immigration, in favour of racial segregation within the country, believe that coloured people are inferior to whites and should be kept in their place, are anti-semitic and generally antagonistic towards people of other races and nationalities. Low scorers, of course, present the opposite pattern of attitudes, being highly tolerant of ethnic minorities, favourable towards coloured immigration, and believing in racial equality. The key to this scale is given below and is used in the same way as the previous one.

2 RACISM

5	+	68	−	147	−
12	+	77	+	155	+
26	+	85	−	165	−
59	+	94	−	174	+
61	+				

The next scale is called religionism, and this is completely self-explanatory. High scorers believe in God, the Bible, life after death and various other supernatural phenomena; they also have favourable attitudes towards the Church and are frequent church attenders. Low scorers are atheist or agnostic in their beliefs and place little value in the Church as a social institution. In general, women tend to be more religious than men; the reasons for this are not entirely clear but their greater submissiveness and suggestibility may partly account for the difference.

3 RELIGIONISM

4	−	50	+	120	−
14	+	66	−	129	+
23	−	93	−	138	−
33	+	102	−		
43	−	111	+		

Factor four is called socialism. High scorers show favourable attitudes towards working-class people and resentment towards wealthy, upper-class people; they favour internationalism and the abolition of private property. Low scores indicate a 'capitalistic' orientation: a belief that talent and enterprise should be well rewarded, that nationalization is inefficient and that worker power is seditious. Clearly this factor relates to social class and voting behaviour.

4 SOCIALISM

6	+	55	+	127	−
15	−	61	−	130	−
16	−	69	−	132	−
20	−	72	+	133	+
24	−	73	+	134	+
25	+	78	+	136	+
26	−	79	−	139	+
29	−	88	−	142	−
30	−	90	−	149	+
31	−	95	−	151	−
34	−	99	−	156	+
35	+	104	+	160	−
44	+	109	−	166	−
47	−	113	−	167	+
52	+	117	+	168	+
53	−	121	+	175	+
54	+	125	−		

The fifth factor has been called libertarianism. High scorers place great value on freedom of the individual and are opposed to almost any kind of interference from the State. Low scorers favour state regulation of both big business and many aspects of individual behaviour; they also place a high stress on patriotism and loyalty to the State.

5 LIBERTARIANISM

6	−	51	+	108	−
11	+	64	−	116	−
17	+	70	+	122	+
18	+	74	+	125	+
20	+	78	+	126	+
24	−	84	−	140	+
37	−	86	+	169	−
41	+	95	+		

The sixth factor in social attitudes is called reactionism. High scorers are greatly disturbed by what they see as moral decay in society. They show strong support for traditional institutions such as the Church and look to the past for their model of life. Low scorers believe that life is changing for the better and show a progressive, future-oriented value system. This scale has a fairly high correlation with age (older people being more 'reactionary') and a strong reverse association with permissiveness (reactionary people are most unlikely to score high on permissiveness).

6 REACTIONISM

8	+	45	+	119	−
20	+	46	+	124	+
32	+	49	+	128	+
33	+	58	−	137	−
38	−	71	−	145	+
42	−	75	+	176	+

The last of the fairly specific attitude factors has been called pacifism. High scorers believe that there is no justification for war; they would prefer a policy of non-violence whatever the cost might be. Low scorers favour the maintenance of military strength and an aggressive policy toward potential belligerents; they believe that war is inherent in human nature, that private persons should have the right to carry arms, and that conscientious objectors are cowards or traitors. Generally speaking, women tend to be more peaceful than men.

7 PACIFISM

2	+	62	–	101	+
3	+	65	+	110	–
7	+	83	–	118	+
13	–	91	–	162	–
22	+	92	–	172	+
27	–				

NEUTRAL

Permissiveness — **Strictness**

146 142 138 134 130 126 122 118 114 110 106 102 98 94 | 90 86 82 78 74 70 66 62 58 54 50 46 42 38 34 30

Racism — **Anti-racism**

65 64 63 62 60 58 56 54 52 50 48 46 44 42 40 | 38 36 34 32 30 28 26 24 22 20 18 16 15 14 13

Religionism — **Non-religionism**

65 64 63 62 60 58 56 54 52 50 48 46 44 42 40 | 38 36 34 32 30 28 26 24 22 20 18 16 15 14 13

Socialism — **Capitalism**

230 225 220 215 210 205 200 195 190 185 180 175 170 165 160 155 | 150 145 140 135 130 125 120 115 110 105 100 95 90 85 80 75

Libertarianism — **Anti-libertarianism**

116 113 110 107 104 101 98 95 92 88 85 82 79 76 73 70 | 67 64 61 58 55 52 49 46 43 40 37 34 32 28 25 22

Reactionism — **Progressivism**

86 84 82 80 78 76 74 72 70 68 66 64 62 60 58 56 | 54 52 50 48 46 44 42 40 38 36 34 32 30 28 26 24

Pacifism — **Militarism**

78 76 74 72 70 68 66 64 62 60 58 56 54 52 50 48 | 46 44 42 40 38 36 34 32 30 28 26 24 22 20 18 16

These seven attitude factors can be collapsed into two very broad 'superfactors' called radicalism-conservatism and tough-mindedness-tendermindedness. The meaning of these factors was outlined in the introduction and it will become much clearer when it is seen how the seven more specific factors combine to produce them. Very briefly, radicals tend to be progressive and socialistic; conservatives favour a traditional viewpoint on most matters and a capitalist economic system. Toughminded attitudes reflect the personality characteristic of the same name; they are strong, masculine and aggressive, as against tenderminded attitudes which are gentle, humane and empathetic.

The two major attitude factors are almost completely independent. That is, being given a score on one of them tells you nothing about what the person is likely to score on the other. This makes it possible to represent them as two axes drawn at right angles as in the diagram below.

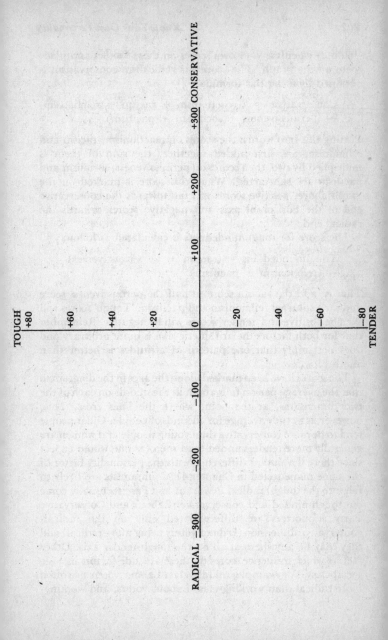

You may calculate your own scores on these factors and place them on the graph. The score for radicalism-conservatism is obtained by using this formula:

Conservatism = 2(reactionism + racism + religionism)
— (permissiveness + socialism + pacifism)

Putting this into words: the scores on reactionism, racism and religionism are first added together, the sum of them is multiplied by two, then scores on permissiveness, socialism and pacifism are subtracted. When this score is marked on the graph above, positive scores will fall towards the conservative end of the horizontal axis and negative scores towards the radical end.

The score for toughmindedness is calculated as follows:

Toughmindedness = (racism + ½ permissiveness)
— (religionism + pacifism)

That is, add the racism score to half the permissiveness score and then subtract religionism and pacifism. 'Tough' scores will then be positive and 'tender' scores will be negative. Remember that for both factors the arithmetic sign is quite arbitrary and does not imply that one pattern of attitudes is better than another.

The scores have been marked along the axes in the diagram so that the average person falls about in the middle on each of the two dimensions, at the point where the lines cross. This, however, is a crude average for all kinds of people. Older people tend to be more conservative than young people and women are generally more tenderminded than men (as one would expect since there is a similar difference with the personality factor of the same name tested in Chapter 4). Communists are likely to fall into the tough/radical quadrant and Fascists usually come out toughminded and conservative. Labour and Conservative Party supporters are differentiated only on the radical-conservative dimension (Labour voters being more radical) and they may be anywhere at all on the tough-tender axis. Other factors which influence scores on these attitude factors include social class. For example, middle-class Labour voters are often more radical than working-class Labour voters, and working-class people who vote for the Conservative Party are frequently more conservative in our sense of the word than middle-class Tories. The reader may amuse himself by speculating as to the likely positions on our graph of various celebrities.

8 | NOW YOU KNOW YOURSELF. . . .

If you have followed faithfully the instructions, have filled in all the questionnaires, scored them carefully, and put your scores into the various profiles, you should be now have a pretty good idea of what your personality is like. If this does nothing else, it should increase your insight; indeed, the major purpose of writing this book was to enable people to gain some insight into their temperament. Unfortunately we have not found it possible to include a questionnaire measure of insight; by definition, such a thing is impossible! Lack of insight is unfortunately very common; it is one of those things your best friend will not tell you. There is a famous instance of lack of insight in Gilbert and Sullivan's *Princess Ida*; remember King Gama's song (which in fact contains Gilbert's jocular self-description):

If you give me your attention, I will tell you what I am:
I'm a genuine philanthropist—all other kinds are sham.
Each little fault of temper and each social defect
In my erring fellow-creatures I endeavour to correct.
To all their little weaknesses I open people's eyes;
And little plans to snub the self-sufficient I devise;
I love my fellow-creatures—I do all the good I can—
Yet everybody says I'm such a disagreeable man!
        And I can't think why!

To compliments inflated I've a withering reply;
And vanity I always do my best to mortify;
A charitable action I can skilfully dissect;
And interested motives I'm delighted to detect;
I know everybody's income and what everybody earns;
And I carefully compare it with the income tax returns;

But to benefit humanity however much I plan,
Yet everybody says I'm such a disagreeable man!
And I can't think why!

I'm sure I'm no ascetic; I'm as pleasant as can be;
You'll always find me ready with a crushing repartee,
I've an irritating chuckle, I've a celebrated sneer,
I've an entertaining snigger, I've a fascinating leer.
To everybody's prejudice I know a thing or two;
I can tell a woman's age in half a minute—and I do.
But although I try to make myself as pleasant as I can,
Yet everybody says I am a disagreeable man!
And I can't think why!

Whether you will like what you find we cannot of course predict. But in case you are one of those people who suffer from feelings of inferiority, and who may be depressed by finding that their self-picture, as it emerges from this book, is not as beautiful as they might have hoped, remember the wise words of Edward Wallis Hoch:

There is so much good in the worst of us,
And so much bad in the best of us,
That it hardly becomes any of us
To talk about the rest of us.

Or, as the author of a more modern version put it: 'Each one of us is a mixture of good qualities and some perhaps not-so-good qualities. In considering our fellow man we should remember his good qualities and realize that his faults only prove that he is, after all, a human being. We should refrain from making harsh judgments of a person just because he happens to be a dirty, rotten, no-good son of a bitch!' This thought applies to ourselves as well as to other people—we are neither as good as we would like to be, nor as bad as we fear we may be, but inherit a mixture of good and bad qualities which are often the reverse sides of the same medal.

We can put these poetic thoughts into a more scientific framework by looking at some genetic facts. The major personality factors we have been dealing with in this book fail to show any evidence of dominance when studied from the genetic point of view; in this they differ strongly from intelligence, which does show directional dominance (in the sense that high intelligence is dominant over low intelligence). In common sense terms, all this means that there is no *biological* advantage in being at one extreme rather than the other of any of our personality factors, whereas there is a biological advantage in being at the high extreme, rather than the low extreme, of the intelligence continuum. Thus there is nothing good or bad in principle in any particular personality pattern you may emerge with; there are advantages and disadvantages attached to all possible combinations. This is worth remembering on occasions when you envy someone else his quick repartee, or his emotional intensity, or his insouciance; he may envy you your reliability, your sang-froid, or your stability.

But most of all, when the simple 'otherness' of other people annoys you, remember that biologically this very diversity—in personality, in temperament, in mental ability, in character, in viewpoint and attitude—is the great strength of our species. Conditions are constantly changing, requiring constant adaptation; what is favourable to adaptation to one set of circumstances may not be favourable to adaptation to another set of circumstances. Our diversity ensures our future survival and success; there is an infinitely varied gene pool from which to draw when humanity encounters adversity and change. Any lessening in this diversity would be a disaster; just those genes which may be needed in the future may be the ones which are being lost. Perhaps this thought may also breed more tolerance of other people; a healthy society needs poets as well as soldiers, bankers as well as sportsmen, musicians as well as miners. A truly homogeneous society, with everyone like everybody else, would be an abomination, short-lived, unstable, and horrid to live in. Let us be grateful for our diversity, and proud to contribute our little bit of different segregation of genes to the total diversity so characteristic of our society.